PENGUIN TWENTIETH-CENTURY CLASSICS

ANNA AKHMATOVA: SELECTED POEMS

Anna Akhmatova was born in 1889 in Odessa on the Black Sea coast. Her early life was spent at Tsarskoye Selo, the imperial summer residence. In 1910 she married Nikolai Gumilev, who was a poet and leader of the 'Acmeist' poetic movement. In 1921 he was shot as an alleged counter-revolutionary; although Anna Akhmatova had been divorced from him for three years, her reputation was to remain tainted by this event, and she published very little of her poetry in the years 1923 to 1940. Her son was arrested and sent to a labour camp, as was her lover, Nikolai Punin, who was released after the death of Stalin.

She remained in Leningrad during the siege but was later evacuated to Tashkent. Her collected works were due for publication in 1945 but never appeared. During this time she was persecuted, expelled from the Writer's Union and followed by two secret police agents. In the thaw after Stalin's death her poetry began to be published again, and when she was allowed to visit the West she received an honorary D.Litt. from Oxford in 1965. She died in 1966.

D. M. Thomas was born in Cornwall in 1935. He is the author of eight novels, including *The White Hotel*, *Ararat* and *Swallow*; six verse collections, including *Dreaming in Bronze* and *Selected Poems*; and four volumes of verse translation, including *The Bronze Horseman: Selected Poems of Pushkin*. He lives in Cornwall.

ANNA AKHMATOVA
SELECTED POEMS

Translated by D. M. Thomas

PENGUIN BOOKS

PENGUIN BOOKS

Published by the Penguin Group
Penguin Books Ltd, 27 Wrights Lane, London W8 5TZ, England
Penguin Books USA Inc., 375 Hudson Street, New York, New York 10014, USA
Penguin Books Australia Ltd, Ringwood, Victoria, Australia
Penguin Books Canada Ltd, 10 Alcorn Avenue, Toronto, Ontario, Canada M4V 3B2
Penguin Books (NZ) Ltd, 182–190 Wairau Road, Auckland 10, New Zealand

Penguin Books Ltd, Registered Offices: Harmondsworth, Middlesex, England

Translation of *Requiem* and *Poem Without a Hero* first published in Great Britain
by Elek Books 1976
Translation of *Way of all the Earth* first published in Great Britain by Martin Secker &
Warburg Ltd 1979
This selection first published, under the title *You Will Hear Thunder*, in Great Britain
by Martin Secker & Warburg Ltd 1985
Published in Penguin Books 1988

7 9 10 8

Printed in England by Clays Ltd, St Ives plc

Contents

By the Seashore

from *White Flock*

from *Plantain*

from *Anno Domini*

from *Reed*

* Poems not published in the collection but written in the same epoch.

Acknowledgements

In the spirit of an apprentice painter joining a master's workshop, I have had three spells of translating Akhmatova: in 1964 (*Requiem*), 1974 (*Poem without a Hero*), and 1977 (a selection of mostly shorter poems). The first two works were published together as *Requiem & Poem without a Hero* (Elek. London, and Ohio U.P., 1976); the third body of translations was published under the title *Way of All the Earth* (Secker & Warburg Ltd., London, and Ohio U.P., 1979). The first of these volumes has long been out of print in Britain, and I am grateful to my publishers for providing an opportunity, in the present book, of bringing all my translations of Akhmatova together.

Akhmatova once referred to 'the blessedness of repetition'. At the risk of some *clumsiness* of repetition (particularly in the Introductions) I have decided to leave the 1976 and 1979 texts essentially as they were.

My primary text was the two-volume *Akhmatova: Sochineniya* (Inter-Language Literary Associates, second edition, 1967–68), edited by G. P. Struve and B. A. Fillipov. I am grateful also to Professor Struve for helpful advice in correspondence. My introduction and notes to *Poem without a Hero* draw heavily on their scholarship, and also on the late Max Hayward's excellent introduction and notes in *Poems of Akhmatova*, selected and translated by Stanley Kunitz with Max Hayward (Collins-Harvill, 1974).

Amanda Haight's biography (*Akhmatova, A Poetic Pilgrimage*, Oxford U.P., 1976) was invaluable in supplying background information and interpretative comment. To her

own translations and to those of Richard McKane and
Stanley Kunitz, I am indebted for the occasions when a
phrase or a line, in one or other of them, struck me as so
'happy' that it would have been foolish to try to find a
better.

I am grateful to Jennifer Munro for her patient help with
texts I found difficult to understand. Michael Glenny and
Vera Dixon also gave me much-appreciated help.

But the errors, both linguistic and aesthetic, are mine;
and the successes—Akhmatova's.

D.M.T.
1984

Introduction

Akhmatova hated the word poetess. If we call her by that name, it is in no condescending sense but from a conviction shared by many critics and readers that her womanliness is an essential element of her poetic genius, a something added, not taken away. Gilbert Frank has pointed to her unusual blending of classical severity and concreteness with lyrical saturation; Andrei Sinyavsky, to the range of her voice 'from the barest whisper to fiery eloquence, from downcast eyes to lightning and thunderbolts'. No insult is intended, therefore, in saying that Akhmatova is probably the greatest poetess in the history of Western culture.

She was born in 1889, in Odessa on the Black Sea coast, but her parents soon moved to Petersburg. All her early life was spent at Tsarskoye Selo, the imperial summer residence; her poetry is steeped in its memories, and in Pushkin, who attended school there. In 1910 she married the poet Nikolai Gumilev, and her own first collection, *Evening*, appeared in 1912. She and her husband became a part of that rich flowering of creative talent—the names Blok, Stravinsky, Diaghilev, Mendelstam Prokofiev, Meyerhold merely begin the list—which made it the Silver Age: though it might better be described as the second Golden Age. Akhmatova, Mandelstam and Gumilev became the leaders of 'Acmeism', a poetic movement which preferred the virtues of classicism, firmness, structure, to the apocalyptic haze and ideological preoccupations of Blok and the other Symbolists.

Gumilev was shot by the Bolsheviks in 1921 as an alleged counter-revolutionary. Despite the fact that Akhmatova and he had been divorced for three years, the taint of having been associated with him never left her. To borrow Pasternak's metaphor (from *Doctor Zhivago*), she had reached the corner of Silver Street and Silent Street: practically none of her poetry was published between 1923 and 1940. At the beginning of the Stalinist Terror, her son, Lev Gumilev, was arrested—released—rearrested, and sent to the labour camps. Nikolai Punin, an art critic and historian, with whom she had been living for ten years, was also arrested, though he was released a year or two later: the first lyric of *Requiem* is said to refer to his arrest. Her son was released early in the war to fight on the front-line; but he was again arrested and transported to Siberia in 1949. He was finally freed only in 1956, after Stalin's death and partial denunciation.

For Akhmatova herself, life was relatively happier during the war, when the enemy was known and could be fought. Such 'happiness', as she said, was a comment on the times! She endured the first terrible months of the Leningrad siege, and was then evacuated, with other artists, to Tashkent. Some of her poems were published, and in 1945 a collected works was said to be forthcoming. It never appeared. In the renewed repression a violent campaign of abuse was directed at her. She was too personal, too mystical. Zhdanov, Stalin's cultural hack, described her as a nun and a whore. This would appear to be a marvellous mixture of archetypes for a poet, but of course his remarks were neither meant, nor taken, in that way. She was expelled from the Writers' Union—tantamount to her abolition—and was henceforth followed everywhere by two secret police agents.

The 'thaw' following Stalin's death led to a cautious rehabilitation. Some of Akhmatova's poetry was published again, though (and this is still the case) never *Requiem*, except in isolated fragments. *Poem without a Hero*, also, has never been published complete in the Soviet Union. Granted permission to visit the West, she received the honorary degree of D.Litt. at Oxford in 1965, and revisited old friends in London and Paris. What was much more important to her than official tolerance, she had become deeply loved and revered by her countrymen. To them, she was the conscience of Russia; she had not fled to safety as others had done after the Revolution; she had chosen to stay and endure, and to 'bear witness'. She died in 1966. Five thousand people, mostly the young, crowded to her requiem mass in a Leningrad church.

Requiem needs little introduction; it speaks for itself. It belongs to a select number of sacred texts which, like American Indian dream-poems but for more sinister reasons, were considered too momentous, too truthful, to write down. From 1935–40, the period of its composition, to 1957, it is said to have survived only in the memories of the poet and a few of her most trusted friends. It was first published in 1963, 'without the author's knowledge or consent', by the Society of Russian Emigré Writers, from a copy which had found its way to the West.

Faced with the events of the Stalinist Terror—the most monstrous epoch in human history, as Joseph Brodsky has called it—only the bravest and most complete artists can respond with anything but silence. For those few who can speak about such things, only two ways of dealing with the horror seem possible: through a relentless piling-on of detail, as Solzhenitsyn has done in *Gulag Archipelago*; or through the intensity of understatement. The latter is *Requiem*'s way. In telling us about one woman, standing in the endless queue outside a Leningrad prison, month after month, hoping to hand in a parcel or hear some news of her son, Akhmatova speaks for all Russia. She achieves universality, through an exquisiteness of style that is at the same time anonymous and transparent—the voice of 'the orphans, the widows', in Chukovsky's prophetic phrase of 1921. *Requiem* honours poetry, as well as the dead.

Though it was slowly distilled, it comes to us as a single heart-rending cry. *Poem without a Hero*, in contrast, is sustained, polyphonic, symphonic. It is a fairly long poem; nevertheless Akhmatora's preoccupation with it over so many years—from 1940 virtually until her death—is astonishing. A poem which describes possession, it possessed her. She writes: 'For fifteen years, again and again, this poem would suddenly come over me, like bouts of an incurable illness (it happened everywhere:

3

listening to music at a concert, in the street, even in my sleep), and I could not tear myself away from it, forever making amendments or additions to a thing that was supposedly finished.' Akhmatova regarded it as her crowning achievement, the poem in which—in the words of Yeats, whom she resembles in some ways—she had 'hammered her thoughts into unity'.

The theme of the poem first came to her, she tells us, on the night of 27 December 1940, in the form of a ghostly masquerade: her friends from the Petersburg of 1913. The whole poem is a superimposition of joyous, talented, light-hearted Petersburg upon tormented Leningrad—or vice versa, since time becomes illusory, and 'mirror of mirror dreams'; a palimpsest of city upon city, the Tsarist capital erased and the Soviet city becoming so, under the German onslaught. One thing is very clear: whatever else the poem is, it is Akhmatova's love poem to her city.

That love is a positive and enriching enchantment. But the poem also relates a negative enchantment or obsession: certain personal events of 1913 which Akhmatova faces anew and, by facing them, expiates. These events are related obliquely ('Don't expect my midnight Tale of /Hoffmann to be laid bare . . .').

One of the cultural centres of pre-Revolutionary Petersburg was the Stray Dog, a basement cabaret decorated by a leading set designer, Sergei Sudeikin. It provided a stage for a constellation of poets—Blok, Bely, Kuzmin, Bryusov, Khlebnikov, Mayakovsky, Gumilev, Akhmatova, Yesenin, all read there to large audiences. There were also intimate theatrical performances. The 'events' which make up the narrative framework of Part One of *Poem without a Hero* concern three members of the Stray Dog coterie. One of them is the great Symbolist poet Alexander Blok. Akhmatova, while revering Blok as a poet, not only disliked the whole Symbolist cult but also—as becomes clear in the poem—sensed a demonism in Blok's nature.

The two other main protagonists are less celebrated. Sudeikin's wife, Olga Glebova-Sudeikina, was one of the great beauties of a city which cultivated feminine beauty.

She acted and danced at the Stray Dog productions, and was a great friend of Akhmatova; they lived together in the same house for several years after the Revolution until Sudeikina emigrated to Paris in 1923. She died there shortly after the Second World War. One of her admirers in Petersburg was Vsevolod Knyazev, a young officer in the dragoons who also wrote poetry. On New Year's Eve, 1912, Knyazev discovered that Blok was his rival for Sudeikina's love, and shot himself on the stairway of her house. His pathetic and senseless death is the obsession that the poem brings into the light and 'weeps out'.

Two other characters enter the poem: Mikhail Kuzmin, described as the Aubrey Beardsley of Russian poetry; and Akhmatova herself. Kuzmin's role is of an arch-Satan. Akhmatova's is more mysterious and important; it appears that she took some of the blame for the tragedy, was involved in the affair in a way she felt guilty about. Also, she felt so close to Sudeikina that she regarded her as a 'double'. Though she was only 'pressed against the glass—frost' on the night of Knyazev's suicide, she too is guilty. Nadezhda Mandelstam has this to say about Akhmatova's preoccupation with the double: 'It was something rooted in her psychology, a result of her attitude to people—in whom, as in mirrors, she always sought her own reflection. She looked at people as one might look into a mirror, hoping to find her own likeness and seeing her "double" in everybody. . . . Apart from the element of self-centredness, it was due as well to another quality which she displayed in high degree: a capacity to become so passionately involved in others that she had the need to tie them to herself as closely as possible, to merge herself in them.'[1]

More important than the reasons for her remorse is the fact that in the poem it takes on a Russia-wide significance. The 'Petersburg event' becomes, in her eyes, 'a parable for the sins of a world on which, with the outbreak of war in 1914, a long and terrible retribution began to be enacted' (Max Hayward). We see a somewhat similar parable at work in *Doctor Zhivago*, in Lara's seduction by Komarovsky;

[1] *Hope Abandoned* (Collins-Harvill and Atheneum).

only in Akhmatova the torment and guilt are accepted as her own.

Part One of *Poem without a Hero* is in four sections. The first narrates the appearance of the unwelcome and terrifying masquerade at her apartment in the old Sheremetyev Palace on the Fontanka canal. The second describes the heroine, Sudeikina. The third is an evocation of Petersburg, as 'not the calendar—the existing/Twentieth century drew near'. The fourth relates Knyazev's death. There is a violent change of tone and mood in Part Two, which opens with the author arguing with a modern Soviet editor, who finds the poem incomprehensible and irrelevant to modern times. The real nightmare of Leningrad's present then moves into the foreground. Part Three describes Akhmatova's evacuation from Leningrad to Tashkent. In her flight from her 'dearest, infernal, granite' city, love and guilt are again mixed.

Poem without a Hero is complex; but less so, I think, than many critics imagine. Most of the apparent difficulty lies in the obscurity and privateness of the 1913 events and in the precise details of a long-dead era. Once these are sufficiently elucidated, the poem becomes no more complex than any great poem. That is, its depths are almost limitless, if one goes on exploring them, yet its surface is clear, real, ordered and beautiful, no more and no less mysterious than the view from your window.

Or than the music of Mozart. That analogy, in fact, is a particularly apt one; the poem is musical, Mozartian. From the title-page motto, a quotation from Da Ponte's libretto to Mozart's *Don Giovanni*, the poem is full of musical references. It is composed in symphonic movements. And its metre, triptychs (normally, two rhymed lines with feminine endings followed by a masculine-ended line), gives it a triple-beat rhythm of ferocious energy, dancing lyrically, demoniacally, tragically—how well it suits the masquerade theme—in one uncurbable impulse from beginning to end.

As important as the poem's fascination with doubles (Sudeikina–Akhmatova; Petersburg–Leningrad; past–future, etc.) is its use as a leitmotif of three, the magic number.

Akhmatova hinted at 'threeness' being fundamental to her poem when she described it as a 'box with a triple bottom'. Often we find a major–major–minor pattern in her groups of three: Blok–Sudeikina–Knyazev, as lovers; Blok–Kuzmin–Knyazev, as poets; Knyazev-Sudeikina–mysterious guest, her dedicatees; the three portraits of Sudeikina in theatrical roles: goatlegged nymph–the blunderer–portrait in shadows; cedar–maple–lilac; Goya–Botticelli–El Greco; Chopin–Bach–'my Seventh', which may be the Seventh Symphony of Beethoven or of Shostakovich. In each of these cases, the third element is more tragic or more mysterious, like a minor chord in music. The significance of doubles and threes is suggested even in the metre, triptychs bound into pairs by rhyme.

Our constant awareness of echoes and mirror-images is enhanced—to the Russian ear at least—by innumerable echoes of earlier poets, especially Pushkin and Blok himself. The cultural interpenetration is so dense and complete that it is almost as if the poem is being written, not by an individual, but by a line of poets, a tradition. And this, of course, is a deliberate and profound contradiction of Soviet theology, which dismisses the pre-Revolutionary past as worthless.

Images of darkness, play-acting and illusion dominate Part One—phantoms, midnight, candles, dreams, and above all, masks and mirrors. This world of 1913 is glamorous and beautiful, frivolous and touched with corruption and a death which no-one believes in. Akhmatova loves this world, and scorns it. At the poem's end, after the whole marvellously created shadow world has been exorcised, the terrible truth breaks free: flying east towards Tashkent, Akhmatova sees below her that endless road along which her son, and millions of others, have been driven to the labour camps. Such a tragic moment of revelation and reality exceeds all that art can do; and through her art Akhmatova shares it all with us—agony, recognition, catharsis . . . 'And that road was long—long—long, amidst the/Solemn and crystal/Stillness/Of Siberia's earth.' At this climax, the poem's predominant major–minor progression is, in the deepest sense, reversed, and we are exalted, as we are at the end of *King Lear*. We feel the unmistakable presence of moral greatness as well as great art—or rather, the moral greatness is an essential condition of the artistic greatness, of the simplicity and majesty of the style.

Nadezhda Mandelstam's recent memoir, *Hope Abandoned*, amply and movingly confirms this impression of Akhmatova. The unflinchingly honest strokes of Nadezhda's pen create a portrait of a woman who, besides her genius, had gifts of life-enriching gaiety and loyalty, and a moral strength which suffering only made stronger. Mandelstam himself foresaw this—almost incredibly—even before the Revolution, when he wrote: 'I would say that she is now no ordinary woman; of her it can truly be said that she is "dressed poorly, but of grand mien". The voice of renunciation grows stronger all the time in her verse, and at the moment her poetry bids fair to become a symbol of Russia's grandeur.' His prophecy came true, in more terrible circumstances than he imagined or *could* have imagined.

(1976)

'Who can refuse to live his own life?' Akhmatova once remarked in answer to some expression of sympathy. Her refusal not to live her life made of her one of those few people who have given dignity and meaning to our terrible century, and through whom and for whom it will be remembered. In relation to her, the politicians, the bureaucrats, the State torturers, will suffer the same fate that, in Akhmatova's words, overtook Pushkin's autocratic contemporaries: 'The whole epoch, little by little . . . began to be called the time of Pushkin. All the . . . high-ranking members of the Court, ministers, generals and non-generals, began to be called Pushkin's contemporaries and then simply retired to rest in card indexes and lists of names (with garbled dates of birth and death) in studies of his work. . . . People say now about the splendid palaces and estates that belonged to them: Pushkin was here, or Pushkin was never here. All the rest is of no interest to them.'

Pushkin was the closest of the friends she did not meet even once in her life. He helped her to survive the 1920s and 30s, the first of Akhmatova's long periods of isolation and persecution. Dante, too, was close. And there were friends whom she could meet, including Mandelstam and Pasternak, whose unbreakable integrity supported her own. But no-one could have helped, through thirty years of persecution, war, and persecution, if she had not herself been one of the rare incorruptible spirits.

Her incorruptibility as a person is closely linked to her most fundamental characteristic as a poet: fidelity to things as they are, to 'the clear, familiar, material world'. It was Mandelstam who pointed out that the roots of her poetry are in Russian prose fiction. It is a surprising truth, in view of the supreme musical quality of her verse; but she has the novelist's concern for tangible realities, events in place and time. The 'unbearably white... blind on the white window' of the first lyric in the present selection is unmistakably real; the last, from half-a-century later, her farewell to the earth, sets her predicted death firmly and precisely in 'that day in Moscow', so that her death seems no more important than the city in which it will take place. In the Russian, the precision is still more emphatic and tangible: 'tot moskovskii den'—'that Muscovite day'. In all her life's work, her fusion with ordinary unbetrayable existence is so complete that only the word 'modest' can express it truthfully. When she tells us (*In 1940*), 'But I warn you,/I am living for the last time', the words unconsciously define her greatness: her total allegiance to the life she was in. She did not make poetry out of the quarrel with herself (in Yeats's phrase for the genesis of poetry). Her poetry seems rather to be a transparent medium through which life streams.

Not that Akhmatova was a simple woman. In many ways she was as complex as Tolstoy. She could reverse her images again and again—a woman of mirrors. 'She was essentially a pagan,' writes Nadezhda Mandelstam: like the young heroine of *By the Sea Shore* who runs barefoot on the shore of the Black Sea; but she was also an unswerving, lifelong Christian. She was one of the languid amoral beauties of St Petersburg's Silver Age; and she was the 'fierce and passionate friend who stood by M. with unshakeable loyalty, his ally against the savage world in which we spent our lives, a stern, unyielding abbess ready to go to the stake for her faith' (N. Mandelstam: *Hope Abandoned*). She was sensual and spiritual, giving rise to the caricature that she was half-nun, half-whore, an early Soviet slander dredged up again in 1946, at the start of her second period of ostracism and persecution. Akhmatova was not alone in believing that she had witch-like powers, capable of causing great hurt to people without consciously intending to; she also knew, quite simply, that she carried, in a brutal age, a burden of goodness. This is the Akhmatova who, in a friend's words, could not bear to see another person's suffering, though she bore her own without complaint.

The air of sadness and melancholy in her portraits was a true part of her, yet we have Nadezhda Mandelstam's testimony that she was 'a wonderful, madcap woman, poet and friend ... Hordes of women and battalions of men of the most widely differing ages can testify to her great gift for friendship, to a love of mischief which never deserted her even in her declining years, to the way in which, sitting at table with vodka and *zakuski*, she could be so funny that everybody fell off their chairs from laughter.' Her incomparable gift for friendship, and her difficulties in coping with love, are wryly suggested in the lines 'other women's/ Husbands' sincerest/Friend, disconsolate/Widow of many...' (*That's how I am ...*) Her love for her son is made abundantly clear in the anguish of *Requiem*, her great sequence written during his imprisonment in the late 30s; yet she found the practicalities of motherhood beyond her.

In Akhmatova all the contraries fuse, in the same wonderful way that her genetic proneness to T.B. was controlled, she said, by the fact that she also suffered from Graves' disease, which holds T.B. in check. The contraries have no effect on her wholeness, but they give it a rich mysterious fluid life, resembling one of her favourite images, the willow. They help to give to her poetry a quality that John Bayley has noted, an 'unconsciousness', elegance and sophistication joined with 'elemental force, utterance haunted and Delphic . . . and a cunning which is *chétif*, or, as the Russians say, *zloi*.'*

Through her complex unity she was able to speak, not to a small élite, but to the Russian people with whom she so closely and proudly identified. Without condescension, with only a subtle change of style within the frontiers of what is Akhmatova, she was able to inspire them with such patriotic war-time poems as *Courage*. It is as though Eliot, in this country, suddenly found the voice of Kipling or Betjeman. The encompassing of the serious and the popular within one voice has become impossible in Western culture. Akhmatova was helped by the remarkable way in which twentieth-century Russian poetry has preserved its formal link with the poetry of the past. It has become modern without needing a revolution, and has kept its innocence. In Russian poetry one can still, so to speak, rhyme 'love' with 'dove'.

Akhmatova herself, with her great compeers, Mandelstam, Pasternak and Tsvetaeva, must be accounted largely responsible for the continuity of Russian poetic tradition. Together, they made it possible for the people to continue to draw strength from them. The crowds who swarmed to Akhmatova's funeral, in Leningrad, filling the church and overflowing into the streets, were expressing her country's gratitude. She had kept the 'great Russian word', and the Word, alive for them. She had outlasted her accusers: had so exasperated them that, as she put it, they had all died before her of heart-attacks. Mandelstam had perished in an Eastern camp; Tsvetaeva had been tormented into suicide; Pasternak had died in obloquy; Akhmatova had lived long enough to receive the openly-expressed love of her country-men and to find joy in the knowledge of poetry's endurance. All four had overcome. The officials of Stalin's monolith were retiring 'to rest in card indexes' in studies of their work. It is a momentous thought. Can it be by chance that the worst of times found the best of poets to wage the war for eternal truth and human dignity?

* *TLS*, 16 April 1976.

In this selection of Akhmatova's poetry I have tried to keep as closely to her sense as is compatible with making a poem in English; and the directness of her art encourages this approach. The geniuses of the Russian language and the English language often walk together, like the two 'friendly voices' Akhmatova overhears in *There are Four of Us;* but they also sometimes clash, and there are times when it is a deeper betrayal of the original poem to keep close to the literal sense than it would be to seek an English equivalent —one that preserves, maybe, more of her music, her 'blessedness of repetition'. Striving to be true to Akhmatova implies, with equal passion, striving to be true to poetry. When I have found it necessary to depart from a close translation, I have sought never to betray the tone and spirit of her poem, but to imagine how she might have solved a particular problem had she been writing in English.

Together with my previous volume, versions of *Requiem* and *Poem without a Hero*, the present selection is intended to be sufficiently large and representative to give English-speaking readers a clearer, fuller impression of her work than has previously been available. Whether or not I have been successful in this, I know that my own gain, from studying her poetry so intimately, has been immense, and beyond thanks, but I thank her.

D.M.T.
(1979)

from Evening

The pillow hot
On both sides,
The second candle
Dying, the ravens
Crying. Haven't
Slept all night, too late
To dream of sleep . . .
How unbearably white
The blind on the white window.
Good morning, morning!

1909

Reading Hamlet

A dusty waste-plot by the cemetery,
Behind it, a river flashing blue.
You said to me: 'Go get thee to a nunnery,
Or get a fool to marry you . . .'

Well, princes are good at such speeches,
As a girl is quick to tears,—
But may those words stream like an ermine mantle
Behind him for ten thousand years.

1909, Kiev

Evening Room

I speak in those words suddenly
That rise once in the soul. So sharply comes
The musty odour of an old sachet,
A bee hums on a white chrysanthemum.

And the room, where the light strikes through slits,
Cherishes love, for here it is still new.
A bed, with a French inscription over it,
Reading: 'Seigneur, ayez pitié de nous.'

Of such a lived-through legend the sad strokes
You must not touch, my soul, nor seek to do . . .
Of Sèvres statuettes the brilliant cloaks
I see are darkening and wearing through.

Yellow and heavy, one last ray has poured
Into a fresh bouquet of dahlias
And hardened there. And I hear viols play
And of a clavecin the rare accord .

———————

I have written down the words
I have long not dared to speak.
Dully the head beats,
This body is not my own.

The call of the horn has died.
The heart has the same puzzles.
Snowflakes,—light—autumnal,
Lie on the croquet lawn.

Let the last leaves rustle!
Let the last thoughts languish!
I don't want to trouble
People used to being happy.

Because your lips are yours
I forgive their cruel joke . . .
O, tomorrow you will come
On the first sledge-ride of winter.

The drawing-room candles will glow
More tenderly in the day.
I will bring from the conservatory
A whole bouquet of roses.

1910, Tsarskoye Selo

Memory of sun seeps from the heart.
Grass grows yellower.
Faintly if at all the early snowflakes
Hover, hover.

Water becoming ice is slowing in
The narrow channels.
Nothing at all will happen here again,
Will ever happen.

Against the sky the willow spreads a fan
The silk's torn off.
Maybe it's better I did not become
Your wife.

Memory of sun seeps from the heart.
What is it?—Dark?
Perhaps! Winter will have occupied us
In the night.

1911, Kiev

Song of the Last Meeting

My breast grew cold and numb,
But my feet were light.
On to my right hand I fumbled
The glove to my left hand.

It seemed that there were many steps
—I knew there were only three.
An autumn whisper between the maples
Kept urging: 'Die with me.

Change has made me weary,
Fate has cheated me of everything.'
I answered: 'My dear, my dear!
I'll die with you. I too am suffering.'

It was a song of the last meeting.
Only bedroom-candles burnt
When I looked into the dark house,
And they were yellow and indifferent.

1911, Tsarskoye Selo

He loved three things alone:
White peacocks, evensong,
Old maps of America.
He hated children crying,
And raspberry jam with his tea,
And womanish hysteria.
. . . And he had married me.

1911

Imitation of Annensky

And with you, my first vagary,
I parted. In the east it turned blue.
You said simply: 'I won't forget you.'
I didn't know at first what you could mean.

Rise and set, the other faces,
Dear today, and tomorrow gone.
Why is it that at this page
Alone the corner is turned down?

And eternally the book opens
Here, as if it's the only part
I must know. From the parting moment
The unreturning years haven't departed.

O, the heart is not made of stone
As I said, it's made of flame . . .
I'll never understand it, are you close
To me, or did you simply love me?

——————

I came here in idleness.
It's all the same where to be bored!
A small mill on a low hilltop.
The years can be silent here.

Softly the bee swims
Over dry convolvulus.
At the pond I call the mermaid
But the mermaid is dead.

The wide pond has grown shallow
And clogged with a rusty slime.
Over the trembling aspen
A light moon shines.

I notice everything freshly.
The poplars smell of wetness.
I am silent. Without words
I am ready to become you again, earth.

1911, Tsarskoye Selo

White Night

I haven't locked the door,
Nor lit the candles,
You don't know, don't care,
That tired I haven't the strength

To decide to go to bed.
Seeing the fields fade in
The sunset murk of pine-needles,
And to know all is lost,

That life is a cursed hell:
I've got drunk
On your voice in the doorway.
I was sure you'd come back.

1911, Tsarskoye Selo

Legend on an Unfinished Portrait

There's nothing to be sad about.
Sadness is a crime, a prison.
A strange impression, I have risen
From the grey canvas like a sheet.

Up-flying arms, with a bad break,
Tormented smile—I and the sitter
Had to become thus through the bitter
Hours of profligate give and take.

He willed it that it should be so,
With words that were sinister and dead.
Fear drove into my lips the red,
And into my cheeks it piled the snow.

No sin in him. I was his fee.
He went, and arranged other limbs,
And other draperies. Void of dreams,
I lie in mortal lethargy.

1912

from Rosary

—'I have come to take your place, sister,
At the high fire in the forest's heart.

Your eyes have grown dull, your tears cloudy,
Your hair is grey.

You don't understand the songs birds sing
Anymore, nor stars, nor summer lightning.

Don't hear it when the women strike
The tambourine; yet you fear the silence.

I have come to take your place, sister,
At the high fire in the forest's heart'. . .

—'You've come to put me in the grave.
Where is your shovel and your spade?
You're carrying just a flute.
I'm not going to blame you,
Sadly a long time ago
My voice fell mute.

Have my clothes to wear,
Answer my fears with silence,
Let the wind blow

Through your hair, smell of the lilac.
You have come by a hard road
To be lit up by this fire.'

And one went away, ceding
The place to another, wandered
Like a blind woman reading
An unfamiliar narrow path,

And still it seemed to her a flame
Was close. . . In her hand a tambourine . . .
And she was like a white flag,
And like the light of a beacon.

1912

For M. Lozinsky

It goes on without end—the day, heavy and amber!
How impossible is grief, how vain the waiting!
And with a silver voice, again the deer
Speaks in the deer-park of the Northern Lights.
And I believe that there is cool snow,
And a blue font for those whose hands are empty,
And a small sledge is being wildly ridden,
Under the ancient chimes of distant bells.

1912

We're all drunkards here. Harlots.
Joylessly we're stuck together.
On the walls, scarlet
Flowers, birds of a feather,

Pine for clouds. Your black pipe
Makes strange shapes rise.
I wear my skirt tight
To my slim thighs.

Windows tightly shut.
What's that? Frost? Thunder?
Did you steal your eyes, I wonder,
From a cautious cat?

O my heart, how you yearn
For your dying hour . . .
And that woman dancing there
Will eternally burn.

1 January 1913

A Ride

My feather was brushing the top of the carriage
And I was looking into his eyes.
There was a pining in my heart
I could not recognize.

The evening was windless, chained
Solidly under a cloudbank,
As if someone had drawn the Bois de Boulogne
In an old album in black indian ink.

A mingled smell of lilac and benzine,
A peaceful watchfulness.
His hand touched my knees
A second time almost without trembling.

1913, May

Nobody came to meet me
    with a lantern,
Had to find my way up
    the steps by weak moonlight

And there he was, under
    the green lamp, and
With a corpse's smile
    he whispered, 'Your voice

Is strange, Cinderella . . .'
    Fire dying in the hearth,
Cricket chirping. Ah!
    someone's taken my shoe

As a souvenir, and with
    lowered eyes given me
Three carnations.
    Dear mementoes,

Where can I hide you?
    And it's a bitter thought
That my little white shoe
    will be tried by everyone.

1913

So many requests, always, from a lover!
None when they fall out of love.
I'm glad the water does not move
Under the colourless ice of the river.

And I'll stand—God help me!—on this ice,
However light and brittle it is,
And you . . . take care of our letters,
That our descendants not misjudge us,

That they may read and understand
More clearly what you are, wise, brave.
In your glorious biography
No row of dots should stand.

Earth's drink is much too sweet,
Love's nets too close together.
May my name be in the textbooks
Of children playing in the street.

When they've read my grievous story,
May they smile behind their desklids . . .
If I can't have love, if I can't find peace,
Give me a bitter glory.

1913

The Voice of Memory

For O. A. Glebova-Sudeikina

What do you see on the wall, your eyes screwed up
When in the sky the sunset's burning late?

Do you see a seagull on the water's blue
Cloth, or gardens by the Arno?

Or the great lake of Tsarskoye Selo
Where terror stepped in front of you?

Or the young man who left your captivity, left
You by walking into death like a white night?

No, I am looking only at the wall's
Reflections of the dying heavenly fires.

1913, June, Slepnyovo

8 November 1913

The sun fills my room,
Yellow dust drifts aslant.
I wake up and remember:
This is your saint's day.

25

That's why even the snow
Outside my window is warm,
Why I, sleepless, have slept
Like a communicant.

8 November 1913

Blue heaven, but the high
Catholic domes are more blue.
Forgive me, happy boy,
The death I brought you.

For the roses from the stall,
For the foolish letters you sent,
That your dark and impudent
Face grew pale.

I thought, a cadet's pride
At becoming adult.
I thought, objects of the cult
Aren't loved like brides.

But it happened to be real.
Into the freezing days,
Already listless, you followed me
Everywhere and always.

As though you wanted to see
Court-evidence
I didn't love you. Forgive me!
Vowed yourself to martyrdom.

And death held out his hand to you . . .
But why? Why did you take it?
I didn't know how frail the naked
Throat under the high blue

Collar. Happy boy . . . tortured
Owlet . . . Forgive me.
I find it hard today
To leave the church.

1913, November

Do you forgive me these November days?
In canals around the Neva fires fragment.
Scant is tragic autumn's finery.

1913, November, Petersburg

The Guest

Nothing is different: thin snow beats
Against the dining-room window-pane.
I am totally unchanged,
But a man came to see me.

I asked: 'What do you want?'
He said: 'To be with you in hell.'
I laughed, 'Ah, there I can't
Oblige you, you'd wish us ill.'

His dry hand touched a petal
With a light caress.
'Tell me how they kiss you,
Tell me how you kiss.'

And his eyes, glinting dully,
Never slid from my ring;
Never a single muscle
Moved under his snakeskin.

O I know: his joy, his greed,
Is to know intensely, eye to eye,
There's nothing that he needs,
Nothing I can deny.

1 January 1914

I won't beg for your love: it's laid
Safely to rest, let the earth settle . . .
Don't expect my jealous letters
Pouring in to plague your bride.
But let me, nevertheless, advise you:
Give her my poems to read in bed,
Give her my portraits to keep—it's wise to
Be kind like that when newly-wed.
For it's more needful to such geese
To know that they have won completely
Than to have converse light and sweet or
Honeymoons of remembered bliss. . .
When you have spent your kopeck's worth
Of happiness with your new friend,
And like a taste that sates the mouth
Your soul has recognized the end—
Don't come crawling like a whelp
Into my bed of loneliness.
I don't know you. Nor could I help.
I'm not yet cured of happiness.

1914

For Alexander Blok

I came to him as a guest.
Precisely at noon. Sunday.
In the large room there was quiet,
And beyond the window, frost

And a sun like raspberry
Over bluish-grey smoke-tangles.
How the reticent master
Concentrates as he looks!

His eyes are of the kind that
Nobody can forget. I'd
Better look out, better
Not look at them at all.

But I remember our talk,
Smoky noon of a Sunday,
In the poet's high grey house
By the sea-gates of the Neva.

1914, January

By the Seashore

I

Bays broke the low shore,
Boats ran out to sea,
And I'd dry my salty hair
On a flat rock a mile from land.
Swam to me the green fish,
Flew to me the white seagull,
I was gay, and bold, and wicked,
And never knew I was happy.
Buried my check dress in sand
That the wind not take it, nor the tramp,
And swam far out to sea,
Rested on the dark warm waves.
Returning, I could see to the east
The regular pulse of the lighthouse,
And a monk at the gates of the
Chersonese said: 'Why are you out at night?'

Neighbours knew I divined water,
And if they dug a new well
They called me to find the spot
To spare them useless work.
I collected French bullets
Instead of mushrooms or bilberries

And carried home in my skirt
The rusty splinters of heavy shells.
And I said to my sister:
'When I become Tsarina
I will build six battleships
And six gunboats
To protect my bays
Right down to Cape Fiolent.'
Evenings, beside the bed,
I'd pray to the dark ikon
That hail would spare the cherries,
That the huge fish would be caught,
That the crafty tramp
Wouldn't find my check dress.

I was friendly with the fishermen,
Under an upturned boat often
When the rain pelted sat with them,
Heard about the sea, and stored it up
In secret, believing every word.
They became used to me.
If I wasn't on the quay
The old fisherman sent a girl
To shout to me: 'Our men are back!
We're frying the flatfish.'

The boy was tall, grey-eyed,
And half a year younger.
He brought me white roses,
White muscat roses,
And asked me gently: 'May I
Sit with you on the rock?'
I laughed: 'What would I do with roses
Except prick myself!' 'If only'
—He replied—'you'd tell me what to do,
I'm so much in love with you.'
I was cross with him: 'Stupid!—
What do you think you are?—Tsarevitch?'
This was the grey-eyed boy

Half a year younger.
'I want to marry you,' he said,
'Soon I'll be grown up
And I'll take you north . . .'
But I didn't want roses
Nor to go north,
So the tall boy started to cry.
        I comforted him badly:
        'Be sensible, I'm going to be
        An empress. Would I want such a
        Husband?' 'Then I'll be a
        Monk, near you in the Chersonese,'
        He said. I said, 'I shouldn't—
        They're always dying when you
        Go there and the rest just stand
        Dry-eyed at the grave.'
He went away without a goodbye,
Clutching his muscat roses,
And I let him go,
I didn't say, 'Stay with me.'
A secret parting pain
Cried like a white gull
Over the grey wormwood steppe,
Over desert, dead Korsun.

2

Bays broke the low shore,
Smoky sun fell in the sea.
Gypsy woman left her cave,
Beckoned me with her finger:
'Why are you walking barefoot,
My lovely? Soon you'll be happy and
Rich. Expect a noble visitor
To call on you before Easter.
Your beauty and your love
Won't tempt him, but your song will.'

I gave the gypsy a small chain
And a small gold christening cross.
Thought joyfully: 'It's the first
News of my beloved from himself.'
But anxiety stopped me loving
My bays and my caves.
I didn't scare the viper in the reeds,
Didn't bring crabs for supper,
But walked along the southern gully
Behind vineyards to the stone-quarry—
That was a long way.
And often the woman
Of the new farm called to me
Distantly: 'Why don't you drop in?
Everybody says you bring good luck.'
I shouted back: 'Only horseshoes
And a new moon bring good luck
—And only if the moon is to your right.'
I didn't like entering rooms.

Blew from the east dry winds,
Large stars fell from the sky,
Church-services were held for sailors
Who had gone to sea,
And jellyfish swam into the bay;
Like stars that had fallen in the night
They gleamed blue, deep underwater.
How cranes coorlee'd in the sky,
How restlessly cicadas chattered,
How the soldier's wife sang her grief—
My keen ears took it all in,
But I knew of no song
To keep my Tsarevitch with me.
I started dreaming of a girl
In narrow bracelets and a short skirt
And a white reed in her cool hands.
Long and peacefully she looks at me,
Doesn't enquire about my sorrow,
Nor talk about her own,

Only tenderly strokes my shoulder.
How will the Tsarevitch know me,
Will he remember my features?
Who will point the way to our house?
Our house is away from the road.

Autumn changed to rainy winter,
Wind blew into the white room
Through open windows. Ivy on the garden
Wall. Strange dogs came to the yard
And howled under my window all night.
It was a bad time for the heart.
So I whispered, looking at the door:
'O God, we will rule wisely,
Build great churches by the sea,
And build tall lighthouses.
We'll take care of water and land,
Nobody shall be harmed.'

3

Dark sea suddenly kinder,
Swallows returning to their nests,
Earth grew red with poppies,
And the shore was good again.
Overnight came the summer—
We didn't see the spring.
I stopped being afraid
My new fate wouldn't come.
On the evening of Palm Sunday,
Coming out of church, I said to my sister:
'I'll leave my candle and beads
And my bible at home for you.
In a week it will be Easter
And it's time I got ready—
I expect the Tsarevitch has left,
He'll be coming for me by sea.'
Silently she wondered at me,

Sighed, doubtless recalled
The gypsy's speech at the cave.
'Is he bringing you a necklace
And a ring with blue stones?'
'No,' I said, 'we don't know
What gift he's planning to give me.'
We were the same age, my sister
And I, and so alike that when
We were small Mama could only tell
Us apart by our birthmarks.
From childhood my sister could not walk,
She lay like a wax doll,
Was never cross with anyone,
Embroidered a holy cloth.
She'd talk about it in her sleep;
I'd hear her murmur:
'The Virgin's cloak will be blue . . .
Lord, I haven't any pearls
For John the Apostle's tears . . .'
The yard grew over with goose-grass and mint,
A donkey nibbled by the wicket-gate,
And on a long wicker armchair
Lay Lena with her arm outstretched,
And as she couldn't work on the holy-day
Worrying about it constantly.
And salt wind brought to us
Easter bells from the Chersonese.
Every clang echoed in my heart
And pulsed with blood along my veins.
'Lenochka,' I said to my sister,
'I'm going down to the shore.
If the Tsarevitch comes
Tell him where to find me.
He can catch me up on the steppe;
Today I must go to the sea.'
'Where did you hear the song
That can lure a Tsarevitch?'
Asked my sister, her eyes half-open:
'You never go to town

And here they don't have such songs.'
I bent till my lips touched her ear
And whispered, 'I'll tell you, Lena,
Actually I thought it up myself,
And there's no better song in the world.'
She did not believe me, and for a long
Time reproached me in silence.

4

Sun baked the well's depths,
Grilled scolopendras on stones,
Tumble-weed ran wild
Like a hunchback clown somersaulting,
And the sky flying high
Was blue as the Virgin's cloak—
Never had been so blue.
Light yachts had afternoon races,
Lazy white sails crowded
Round Constantine's battery—
Evidently the wind veered well.
Slowly I walked along the bay
To the cape, those black broken rocks
Foam covers when the surf comes in,
And I said my new song over.
I knew, whoever the Tsarevitch was with,
My voice would confuse him—
And so every word of it
Was like God's gift, dear to me.
The first yacht didn't sail—flew,
And the second was catching it,
While the rest could hardly be seen.
I don't remember lying by water,
Don't know how I dozed, only
That I woke and saw a sail
Flapping close by. In front of me,
Up to his waist in clear water,
A huge old man scrabbles his arms

In the deep cracks of the shore cliffs,
Hoarsely cries for help.
Loudly I said the prayer
I was taught as a child
To protect me from nightmares,
To keep the house safe.
I got to: 'You who are Saviour!'
I saw something white in
The old man's arms, and my heart froze . . .
The sailor was lifting out the sailor
Of the most joyful and winged ship,
And on dark rocks laid him.

Long I couldn't trust myself,
Bit my finger to wake up:
Dusky and tender my Tsarevitch
Lay quietly and looked at the sky.
His eyes greener than the sea
And darker than our cypresses—
I could see them fading . . .
Better to have been born blind.
He groaned and cried indistinctly:
'Swallow, O swallow, how it hurts!'
It seemed he saw me as a bird.

At dusk I went back home.
In the dark room it was quiet
And over the ikon lamp stood
A high, thin, crimson flame.
'The Tsarevitch didn't come,'
Lena said as she heard steps:
'I waited for him till vespers
And sent the children down to the quay.'
'He won't be coming for me,
He will never come back, Lena.
My Tsarevitch is dead.'
Time and again she crossed herself,
She turned to the wall and was silent.
I could tell that Lena was crying.

I heard that they sang over him
'Christ is risen from the dead'—
And an ineffable light
Shone in the round church.

1914

from White Flock

Loneliness

So many stones are thrown at me,
They no longer scare.
Fine, now, is the snare,
Among high towers a high tower.
I thank its builders: may
They never need a friend.
Here I can see the sun rise earlier
And see the glory of the day's end.
And often into the window of my room
Fly the winds of a northern sea,
A dove eats wheat from my hands . . .
And the Muse's sunburnt hand
Divinely light and calm
Finishes the unfinished page.

Summer 1914 Slepnyovo,

How can you look at the Neva,
Stand on bridges just the same? . . .
No wonder I've borne signs of grieving
Since the night your image came.

Sharp are the black angels' wings,
Soon the judgement of the dead,
And street bonfires blazing red
Like roses in snow are flowering.

1914

The road is black by the beach-
Garden. Lamps yellow and fresh.
I'm very calm.
I'd rather not talk about him.

I've a lot of feeling for you. You're kind.
We'll kiss, grow old, walk around.
Light months will fly over us
Like snowy stars.

1914

Flight

For O. A. Kuzmin-Karavaev

'If we could only reach the shore,
My dear!'—'Sh! Be quiet!'. . .
And we started down the stairs,
Hardly breathing, searching for keys.

Past the house where we had once
Danced and drunk wine,
Past the Senate's white columns
To where it was dark, dark.

'What are you doing? You're mad!'—
'Not mad. In love with you!
This wind is wide and billowing,
Gaily it will take the ship!'

Throat tight with horror,
The canoe took us in the gloom . . .
The tang of an ocean cable
Burnt my trembling nostrils.

'Tell me—if you know yourself:
Am I asleep? Is this a dream? . . .'
Only the oars splashed evenly
Along the heavy Neva wave.

But the black sky grew lighter,
Someone called to us from a bridge.
With both hands I seized the chain
Of the cross on my breast.

Powerless, I was lifted in your arms
Like a young girl on to the deck
Of the white yacht, to meet the light
Of incorruptible day.

1914, Summer

I don't know if you're alive or dead.
Can you on earth be sought,
Or only when the sunsets fade
Be mourned serenely in my thought?

All is for you: the daily prayer,
The sleepless heat at night,
And of my verses, the white
Flock, and of my eyes, the blue fire.

No-one was more cherished, no-one tortured
Me more, not
Even the one who betrayed me to torture,
Not even the one who caressed me and forgot.

1915

There is a frontier-line in human closeness
That love and passion cannot violate—
Though in silence mouth to mouth be soldered
And passionate devotion cleave the heart.

Here friendship, too, is powerless, and years
Of that sublime and fiery happiness
When the free soul has broken clear
From the slow languor of voluptuousness.

Those striving towards it are demented, and
If the line seem close enough to broach—
Stricken with sadness . . . Now you understand
Why my heart does not beat beneath your touch.

1915, May, Petersburg

Freshness of words, simplicity of emotions,
If we lost these, would it not be as though
Blindness had stricken Fra Angelico,
Or an actor lost his power of voice and motion?

But don't behave as if you own
What has been given you by the Saviour:
We ourselves know, we are condemned to squander
Our wealth, and not to save. Alone

Go out and heal the cataract,
And later, witness your own disciples'
Malice and jeers, and see the people's
Stolid indifference to the act.

1915

Under an empty dwelling's frozen roof,
Dead days. Here no living comes.
I read the Acts of the Apostles
And the Psalms.

But the stars are blue, the hoar-frost downy,
And each meeting more wonderful,
And in the Bible a red maple leaf
Marks the pages of the Song of Songs.

1915

The churchyard's quiet on a Sunday,
Under an oak board I shall rest.
Come to me, my dearest, running,
Come to your mama, like a guest.
Over the stream and hillside run,
So the slow grown-ups disappear;
From far, the keen eyes of my son
Will recognize my cross. My dear,
I know I can't expect you to
Remember me, who neither kissed
And dandled you, nor scolded you,
Nor took you to the eucharist.

1915

Neither by cart nor boat
Could you have got here.
On rotten snow
The deep water;
Farmsteads marooned and
Ah! that morose
Soul, that Robinson,
Is so close.
How often can
He inspect sledge and skis,
Return to the divan
To sit and wait for me?
And his short spur grinds
Sheer through the vile
Rug. Now mirrors learn
Not to expect smiles.

1916

Lying in me, as though it were a white
Stone in the depths of a well, is one
Memory that I cannot, will not, fight:
It is happiness, and it is pain.

Anyone looking straight into my eyes
Could not help seeing it, and could not fail
To become thoughtful, more sad and quiet
Than if he were listening to some tragic tale.

I know the gods changed people into things,
Leaving their consciousness alive and free.
To keep alive the wonder of suffering,
You have been metamorphosed into me.

Summer 1916, Slepnyovo

O there are words that should not be repeated,
And he who speaks them—is a spendthrift.
Inexhaustible is the sky's blue spindrift
Alone, and the mercy of the Redeemer.

Winter 1916, Sebastopol

from Plantain

Now farewell, capital,
Farewell, my spring,
Already I can hear
Karelia yearning.

Fields and kitchen-gardens
Are green and peaceful,
The waters are still deep,
And the skies still pale.

And the marsh rusalka,
Mistress of those parts,
Gazes, sighing, up at
The bell-tower cross.

And the oriole, friend
Of my innocent days,
Has flown back from the south
And cries among the branches

That it's shameful to stay
Until May in the cities,
To stifle in theatres,
Grow bored on the islands.

But the oriole doesn't know,
Rusalka won't understand,
How lovely it is
Kissing him!

All the same, right now,
On the day's quiet slope,
I'm going. God's land,
Take me to you!

1917

I hear the oriole's always grieving voice,
And the rich summer's welcome loss I hear
In the sickle's serpentine hiss
Cutting the corn's ear tightly pressed to ear.

And the short skirts of the slim reapers
Fly in the wind like holiday pennants,
The clash of joyful cymbals, and creeping
From under dusty lashes, the long glance.

I don't expect love's tender flatteries,
In premonition of some dark event,
But come, come and see this paradise
Where together we were blessed and innocent.

1917, Summer

Now no-one will be listening to songs.
The days long prophesied have come to pass.
The world has no more miracles. Don't break
My heart, song, but be still: you are the last.

Not long ago you took your morning flight
With all a swallow's free accomplishment.
Now that you are a hungry beggar-woman,
Don't go knocking at the stranger's gate.

1917

The cuckoo I asked
How many years I would live . . . The
Pine tops shivered,
A yellow shaft fell to the grass.
In the fresh forest depths, no sound . . .
I am going
Home, and the cool wind
Caresses my hot brow.

1919, 1 June

Why is our century worse than any other?
Is it that in the stupor of fear and grief
It has plunged its fingers in the blackest ulcer,
Yet cannot bring relief?

Westward the sun is dropping,
And the roofs of towns are shining in its light.
Already death is chalking doors with crosses
And calling the ravens and the ravens are in flight.

1919

from Anno Domini

Everything is looted, spoiled, despoiled,
Death flickering his black wing,
Anguish, hunger—then why this
Lightness overlaying everything?

By day, cherry-scent from an unknown
Wood near the town. July
Holding new constellations, deep
At night in the transparent sky—

Nearer to filthy ruined houses
Flies the miraculous . . .
Nobody has ever known it,
This, always so dear to us.

1921

They wiped your slate
With snow, you're not alive.
Bayonets twenty-eight
And bullet-holes five.
It's a bitter present,
Love, but I've sewed it.
Russia, an old peasant
Killing his meat.

1921

Bezhetsk

There are white churches there, and the crackle of
    icicles,
The cornflower eyes of my son are blossoming there.
Diamond nights above the ancient town, and yellower
Than lime-blossom honey is the moon's sickle.
From plains beyond the river dry snow-storms fly in,
And the people, like the angels in the fields, rejoice.
They have tidied the best room, lit in the icon-case
The tiny lamps. On an oak table the Book is lying.
There stern memory, so ungiving now,
Threw open her tower-rooms to me, with a low bow;
But I did not enter, and I slammed the fearful door;
And the town rang with the news of the Child that
    was born.

                    26 December 1921

To earthly solace, heart, be not a prey,
To wife and home do not attach yourself,
Take the bread out of your child's mouth,
And to a stranger give the bread away.
Become the humblest servant to the man
Who was your blackest enemy,
Call by your brother's name the forest wolf,
And do not ask God for anything.

I'm not of those who left their country
For wolves to tear it limb from limb.
Their flattery does not touch me.
I will not give my songs to them.

Yet I can take the exile's part,
I pity all among the dead.
Wanderer, your path is dark,
Wormwood is the stranger's bread.

But here in the flames, the stench,
The murk, where what remains
Of youth is dying, we don't flinch
As the blows strike us, again and again.

And we know there'll be a reckoning,
An account for every hour . . . There's
Nobody simpler than us, or with
More pride, or fewer tears.

1922

Blows the swan wind,
The blue sky's smeared
With blood; the anniversary
Of your love's first days draws near.

You have destroyed
My sorcery; like water the years
Have drifted by. Why
Aren't you old, but as you were?

Your tender voice even more ringing . . .
Only your serene brow
Has taken from time's wing
A scattering of snow.

1922

To fall ill as one should, deliriously
Hot, meet everyone again,
To stroll broad avenues in the seashore garden
Full of the wind and the sun.

Even the dead, today, have agreed to come,
And the exiles, into my house.
Lead the child to me by the hand.
Long I have missed him.

I shall eat blue grapes with those who are dead,
Drink the iced
Wine, and watch the grey waterfall pour
On to the damp flint bed.

Behind the lake the moon's not stirred
And seems to be a window through
Into a silent, well-lit house,
Where something unpleasant has occurred.

Has the master been brought home dead,
The mistress run off with a lover,
Or has a little girl gone missing,
And her shoes found by the creek-bed . . .

We can't see. But feel some awful thing,
And we don't want to talk.
Doleful, the cry of eagle-owls, and hot
In the garden the wind is blustering.

1922

Rachel

A man met Rachel, in a valley. Jacob
Bowed courteously, this wanderer far from home.
Flocks, raising the hot dust, could not slake their
Thirst. The well was blocked with a huge stone.
Jacob wrenched the stone from the well
Of pure water, and the flocks drank their fill.

But the heart in his breast began to grieve,
It ached like an open wound.
He agreed that in Laban's fields he should serve
Seven years to win the maiden's hand.
For you, Rachel! Seven years in his eyes
No more than seven dazzling days.

But silver-loving Laban lives
In a web of cunning, and is unknown to grace.
He thinks: every deceit forgives
Itself to the glory of Laban's house.
And he led Leah firmly to the tent
Where Jacob took her, blind and innocent.

Night drops from on high over the plains,
The cool dews pour,
And the youngest daughter of Laban groans,
Tearing the thick braids of her hair.
She curses her sister and reviles God, and
Begs the Angel of Death to descend.

And Jacob dreams the hour of paradise:
In the valley the clear spring,
The joyful look in Rachel's eyes,
And her voice like a bird's song.
Jacob, was it you who kissed me, loved
Me, and called me your black dove?

1921

Lot's Wife

And the just man trailed God's messenger,
His huge, light shape devoured the black hill.
But uneasiness shadowed his wife and spoke to her:
'It's not too late, you can look back still

At the red towers of Sodom, the place that bore you,
The square in which you sang, the spinning-shed,
At the empty windows of that upper storey
Where children blessed your happy marriage-bed.'

Her eyes that were still turning when a bolt
Of pain shot through them, were instantly blind;
Her body turned into transparent salt,
And her swift legs were rooted to the ground.

55

Who mourns one woman in a holocaust?
Surely her death has no significance?
Yet in my heart she never will be lost,
She who gave up her life to steal one glance.

1922–24

from Reed

Muse

When at night I wait for her to come,
Life, it seems, hangs by a single strand.
What are glory, youth, freedom, in comparison
With the dear welcome guest, a flute in hand?

She enters now. Pushing her veil aside,
She stares through me with her attentiveness.
I question her: 'And were you Dante's guide,
Dictating the Inferno?' She answers: 'Yes.'

1924

To an Artist

Your work that to my inward sight still comes,
Fruit of your graced labours:
The gold of always-autumnal limes,
The blue of today-created waters—

Simply to think of it, the faintest drowse
Already has led me into your parks
Where, fearful of every turning, I lose
Consciousness in a trance, seeking your tracks.

Shall I go under this vault, transfigured by
The movement of your hand into a sky,
To cool my shameful heat?

There I shall become forever blessed,
There my burning eyelids will find rest,
And I'll regain a gift I've lost—to weep.

1924

The Last Toast

I drink to our demolished house,
To all this wickedness,
To you, our loneliness together,
I raise my glass—

And to the dead-cold eyes,
The lie that has betrayed us,
The coarse, brutal world, the fact
That God has not saved us.

1934

Dust smells of a sun-ray,
Girls' breaths, — violets hold,
Freedom clings to the wild honey,
But there's no smell to gold.

The mignonette smells of water,
Apple-tang clings to love,
But we were always taught that
Blood smells only of blood.

So it was no use the governor from Rome
Washing his hands before the howls
Of the wicked mob,
And it was in vain
That the Scottish queen washed the scarlet
Splashes from her narrow palms
In the thane's gloomy suffocating home.

58

Some gaze into tender faces,
Others drink until morning light,
But all night I hold conversations
With my conscience who is always right.

I say to her: 'You know how tired I am,
Bearing your heavy burden, many years.'
But for her, there is no such thing as time,
And for her, space also disappears.

And again, a black Shrove Tuesday,
The sinister park, the unhurried ring
Of hooves, and, flying down the heavenly
Slopes, full of happiness and joy, the wind.

And above me, double-horned and calm
Is the witness . . . O I shall go there,
Along the ancient well-worn track,
To the deathly waters, where the swans are.

1936

Boris Pasternak

He who compared himself to the eye of a horse,
Peers, looks, sees, recognizes,
And instantly puddles shine, ice
Pines away, like a melting of diamonds.

Backyards drowse in lilac haze. Branch-
Line platforms, logs, clouds, leaves . . .
The engine's whistle, watermelon's crunch,
A timid hand in a fragrant kid glove. He's

Ringing, thundering, grinding, up to his breast
In breakers . . . and suddenly is quiet. . . This means
He is tiptoeing over pine needles, fearful lest
He should startle space awake from its light sleep.

It means he counts the grains in the empty ears,
And it means he has come back
From another funeral, back to Darya's
Gorge, the tombstone, cursed and black.

And burns again, the Moscow tedium,
In the distance death's sleigh-bell rings . . .
Who has got lost two steps from home,
Where the snow is waist-deep, an end to everything?

Because he compared smoke with Laocoön,
Made songs out of graveyard thistles,
Because he filled the world with a sound no-one
Has heard before, in a new space of mirrored

Verses, he has been rewarded with a form
Of eternal childhood, with the stars' vigilant love,
The whole earth has been passed down to him,
And he has shared it with everyone.

19 January 1936

Voronezh

O.M.

And the town is frozen solid, leaden with ice.
Trees, walls, snow, seem to be under glass.
Cautiously I tread on crystals.
The painted sleighs can't get a grip.
And over the statue of Peter-in-Voronezh
Are crows, and poplars, and a pale-green dome
Washed-out and muddy in the sun-motes.
The mighty slopes of the Field of Kulikovo
Tremble still with the slaughter of barbarians.
And all at once the poplars, like lifted chalices,
Enmesh more boisterously overhead
Like thousands of wedding-guests feasting
And drinking toasts to our happiness.

And in the room of the banished poet
Fear and the Muse take turns at watch,
And the night comes
When there will be no sunrise.

1936

Imitation from the Armenian

I shall come into your dream
As a black ewe, approach the throne
On withered and infirm
Legs, bleating: 'Padishah,
Have you dined well? You who hold
The world like a bead, beloved
Of Allah, was my little son
To your taste, was he fat enough?'

1930s

Dante

He did not return, even after his death, to
That ancient city he was rooted in.
Going away, he did not pause for breath
Nor look back. My song is for him.
Torches, night, a last embrace,
Fate, a wild howl, at his threshold.
Out of hell he sent her his curse
And in heaven could not forget her.
But never in a penitential shirt did
He walk with a lighted candle and barefoot
Through beloved Florence he could not betray,
Perfidious, base, and self-deserted.

1936

Cleopatra

I am air and fire . . .

Shakespeare

She has kissed lips already grown inhuman,
On her knees she has wept already before Augustus . . .
And her servants have betrayed her. Under the Roman
Eagle clamour the raucous trumpets, and the dusk has

Spread. And enter the last hostage to her glamour.
'He'll lead me, then, in triumph?' 'Madam, he will.
I know't.' Stately, he has the grace to stammer . . .
But the slope of her swan neck is tranquil still.

Tomorrow, her children . . . O, what small things rest
For her to do on earth—only to play
With this fool, and the black snake to her dark breast
Indifferently, like a parting kindness, lay.

1940

Willow

In the young century's cool nursery,
In its checkered silence, I was born.
Sweet to me was not the voice of man,
But the wind's voice was understood by me.
The burdocks and the nettles fed my soul,
But I loved the silver willow best of all.
And, grateful for my love, it lived
All its life with me, and with its weeping
Branches fanned my insomnia with dreams. But
—Surprisingly enough!—I have outlived
It. Now, a stump's out there. Under these skies,
Under these skies of ours, are other
Willows, and their alien voices rise.
And I am silent . . . As though I'd lost a brother.

1940

In Memory of Mikhail Bulgakov

This, not graveyard roses, is my gift;
And I won't burn sticks of incense:
You died as unflinchingly as you lived,
With magnificent defiance.
Drank wine, and joked—were still the wittiest,
Choked on the stifling air.
You yourself let in the terrible guest

And stayed alone with her.
Now you're no more. And at your funeral feast
We can expect no comment from the mutes
On your high, stricken life. One voice at least
Must break that silence, like a flute.
O, who would have believed that I who have been
    tossed
On a slow fire to smoulder, I, the buried days'
Orphan and weeping mother, I who have lost
Everything, and forgotten everyone, half-crazed—
Would be recalling one so full of energy
And will, and touched by that creative flame,
Who only yesterday, it seems, chatted to me,
Hiding the illness crucifying him.

House on the Fontanka, 1940

When a man dies
His portraits change.
His eyes look at you
Differently and his lips smile
A different smile. I noticed this
Returning from a poet's funeral.
Since then I have seen it verified
Often and my theory is true.

1940

Not the lyre of a lover
I'll carry through my land.
The rattle of a leper
Will sing in my hand.

Way of all the Earth

*And the Angel swore to the living
that there will be no Time . . .*

Revelations

I

Straight in the bullets' flight,
Thrusting aside the years,
Through Januarys and Julys
I shall make my way there . . .
No-one will see the gash,
No-one will hear me moan,
I, the woman of Kitezh,
Have been called home.
Of birchtrees is racing
An uncountable host
After me. A glacier
Is the streaming frost.
Charred is the glade
From an ancient fire.
'Here's my pass, comrade,
Let me through to the rear . . .'
A warrior's decision,
A bayonet turns.
How brilliantly risen,
An island that burns!
Red clay again and
The apple orchard . . .
O, Salve Regina!—
The sunset a torchglow.
The footpath climbs steeply,

A trembling, and
Somebody is needed
To stretch me a hand . . .
But unheard is the harsh
Barrel-organ. It groans,
But the woman of Kitezh
Can hear other sounds.

2

Trenches, and still more—you
Could get lost here!—ahead.
Of ancient Europe
Remains but a shred,
Where in a cloud of smoke
Towns consume,
And there already the dark
Ridge of Crimea looms.
I go with a flock
Of mourners behind.
O blue cloak
Of a quiet land! . . .
By a dead medusa
I stand on the shore;
Here I met the Muse, and
I vow to her once more.
She thinks me a fable,
Laughs loudly: 'Is it you?'
Fragrant April
Lets fall its dew.
Here of glory
Already have dawned
The high portals,
But a sly voice warned:
'You will come back,
Come back many times. And
Each time you will strike
On the hard diamond.

You had better go past,
You had better return,
Cursed, and praised,
To your fathers' garden.'

3

Thickening gloom
Of evening. Why
Doesn't Hoffman come
To the corner with me?
He knows how hollow
Is the muffled cry of pain,
And he knows whose double
Has entered the lane.
It isn't funny
That for twenty five years
The same uncanny
Silhouette appears.
'To the right, do you mean?
Here, round the corner? Thank
You!'—The gleam
Of a ditch, a small
House. I hadn't
Known how the moon's
In everything. By a ladder
Of leaves having swung down
It peacefully crept
Past the forsaken
House where the night's end
At a round table
Gazed into what remained
Of a mirror and on the breast
Of darkness a knifed
Man slept.

Like the high power
Of purest sound,
Separation, you're
Homeward-bound.
Familiar buildings
Look out from death at us—
And there are still things
A hundred times worse
For me to face than all
I faced, that other time . . .
Through my crucified capital
I am going home.

The bird-cherry tree stole
Past like a dream. And
Somebody on the telephone
Said the word 'Tsushima!'
To the dying age. It's
Time to make haste:
The *Varyag* and the *Koreyetz*
Have gone to the east . . .
There we caught
The ancient pain
Of swallows, and then, Fort
Shabrol is darkly seen,
Like the forgotten
Age's ruined vault,
Where an old cripple rots. He's
Deaf and blind. Halt
Before the stern and grim-
Faced Boers whose rifles block
The way, guarding him.
'Get back! Get back!'

For the great
Winter I have waited long,
Like a monk's white
Habit I have put it on.
Calmly I sit in the light
Sledge, and to you, men and women
Of Kitezh, before night
I shall return.
There's one place to cross,
The ancient ferry . . . Now
With the woman of Kitezh
Nobody will go,
Not brother nor neighbour of mine
Will be there, nor my first
Husband—only a pine
Branch and a sunny verse
That I picked up
When a beggar let it fall . . .
In the house where I'll stop,
Repose of my soul.

1940, March, House on the Fontanka

from **The Seventh Book**

In 1940

I

When you bury an epoch
You do not sing psalms at the tomb.
Soon, nettles and thistles
Will be in bloom.
And only—bodies won't wait!—
The gravediggers toil;
And it's quiet, Lord, so quiet,
Time has become audible.
And one day the age will rise,
Like a corpse in a spring river—
But no mother's son will recognize
The body of his mother.
Grandsons will bow their heads.
The moon like a pendulum swinging.

And now—over stricken Paris
Silence is winging.

To the Londoners

Shakespeare's play, his twenty-fourth—
Time is writing it impassively.
By the leaden river what can we,
Who know what such feasts are,
Do, except read Hamlet, Caesar, Lear?
Or escort Juliet to her bed, and christen
Her death, poor dove, with torches and singing;
Or peep through the window at Macbeth,
Trembling with the one who kills from greed—
Only not this one, not this one, not this one,
This one we do not have the strength to read.

3

Shade

*What does a certain woman know
about the hour of her death?*

O. Mandelstam

Tallest, most elegant of us, why does memory
Insist you swim up from the years, pass
Swaying down a train, searching for me,
Transparent profile through the carriage-glass?
Were you angel or bird?—how we argued it!
A poet took you for his drinking-straw.
Your Georgian eyes through sable lashes lit
With the same even gentleness, all they saw.
O shade! Forgive me, but clear sky, Flaubert,
Insomnia, the lilacs flowering late,
Have brought you—beauty of the year
'13—and your unclouded temperate day,
Back to my mind, in memories that appear
Uncomfortable to me now. O shade!

4

I thought I knew all the paths
And precipices of insomnia,
But this is a trumpet-blast
And like a charge of cavalry.
I enter an empty house
That used to be someone's home,
It's quiet, only white shadows
In a stranger's mirrors swim.
And what is that in a mist?—
Denmark? Normandy? or some time
In the past did I live here,
And this—a new edition
Of moments forever lost?

5

But I warn you,
I am living for the last time.
Not as a swallow, not as a maple,
Not as a reed nor as a star,
Not as water from a spring,
Not as bells in a tower—
Shall I return to trouble you
Nor visit other people's dreams
With lamentation.

1940

Courage

We know what trembles in the scales,
What has to be accomplished.
The hour for courage. If all else fails,
With courage we are not unfurnished.

What though the dead be crowded, each to each,
What though our houses be destroyed?—
We will preserve you, Russian speech,
Keep you alive, great Russian word.
We will pass you to our sons and heirs
Free and clean, and they in turn to theirs,
    And so forever.

        1942, 23 February

And you, my friends who have been called away,
I have been spared to mourn for you and weep,
Not as a frozen willow over your memory,
But to cry to the world the names of those who sleep.
What names are those!
      I slam shut the calendar,
Down on your knees, all!
       Blood of my heart,
The people of Leningrad march out in even rows,
The living, the dead: fame can't tell them apart.

          1942

That's how I am. I could wish for you someone other,
Better.
    I trade in happiness no longer . . .
Charlatans, pushers at the sales! . . .
We stayed peacefully in Sochi,
Such nights, there, came to me,
And I kept hearing such bells!
Over Asia were spring mists, and
Tulips were carpeting with brilliance
Several hundreds of miles.
O, what can I do with this cleanness,
This simple untaintable scene? O,
What can I do with these souls!
I could never become a spectator.

I'd push myself, sooner or later,
Through every prohibited gate.
Healer of tender hurts, other women's
Husbands' sincerest
Friend, disconsolate
Widow of many. No wonder
I've a grey crown, and my sun-burn
Frightens the people I pass.
But—like her—I shall have to part with
My arrogance—like Marina the martyr—
I too must drink of emptiness.
You will come under a black mantle,
With a green and terrible candle,
Screening your face from my sight . . .
Soon the puzzle will be over:
Whose hand is in the white glove, or
Who sent the guest who calls by night.

1942, Tashkent

Three Autumns

The smiles of summer are simply indistinct
And winter is too clear,
But I can unerringly pick out
Three autumns in each year.

The first is a holiday chaos
Spiting the summer of yesterday.
Leaves fly like a schoolboy's notes,
Like incense, the smell of smoke,
Everything moist, motley, gay.

First into the dance are the birches,
They put on their transparent attire
Hastily shaking off their fleeting tears
On to the neighbour next door.

73

But as it happens, the story's just begun.
A moment, a minute—and here
Comes the second, passionless as conscience,
Sombre as an air raid.

Everything suddenly seems paler, older,
Summer's comfort is plundered,
Through the scented fog float
Far-off marches played on golden trumpets . . .

A flagstone covers the sky vault. Cold waves
Of incense. But the wind's started to blow
Everything clean open, and straightway
It's clear that this is the end of the play,
This is not the third autumn but death.

1943

The souls of those I love are on high stars.
How good that there is no-one left to lose
And one can weep. Tsarskoye Selo's
Air was made to repeat songs.

By the river bank the silver willow
Touches the bright September waters.
Rising from the past, my shadow
Comes silently to meet me.

So many lyres, hung on branches, here,
But there seems a place even for my lyre.
And this shower, drenched with sun and rare,
Is consolation and good news.

———————

The fifth act of the drama
Blows in the wind of autumn,
Each flower-bed in the park seems
A fresh grave, we have finished

The funeral-feast, and there's nothing
To do. Why then do I linger
As if I am expecting
A miracle? It's the way a feeble
Hand can hold fast to a heavy
Boat for a long time by the pier
As one is saying goodbye
To the person who's left standing.

1921(?)

It is your lynx eyes, Asia,
That spied something in me,
Teased it out, occult
And born of stillness,
Oppressive and difficult
Like the noon heat in Termez.
As though pre-memory's years
Flowed like lava into the mind . . .
As if I were drinking my own tears
From a stranger's cupped hands.

1945

In Dream

Black and enduring separation
I share equally with you.
Why weep? Give me your hand,
Promise me you will come again.
You and I are like high
Mountains and we can't move closer.
Just send me word
At midnight sometime through the stars.

1946

So again we triumph!
Again we do not come!
Our speeches silent,
Our words, dumb.
Our eyes that have not met
Again, are lost;
And only tears forget
The grip of frost.
A wild-rose bush near Moscow
Knows something of
This pain that will be called
Immortal love.

1956

You are with me once more, Autumn my friend!

Annensky

Let any, who will, still bask in the south
On the paradisal sand,
It's northerly here—and this year of the north
Autumn will be my friend.

I'll live, in a dream, in a stranger's house
Where perhaps I have died,
Where the mirrors keep something mysterious
To themselves in the evening light.

I shall walk between black fir-trees,
Where the wind is at one with the heath,
And a dull splinter of the moon will glint
Like an old knife with jagged teeth.

Our last, blissful unmeeting I shall bring
To sustain me here—
The cold, pure, light flame of conquering
What I was destined for.

1957

from Northern Elegies

The Fifth

I, like a river,
Have been turned aside by this harsh age.
I am a substitute. My life has flowed
Into another channel
And I do not recognize my shores.
O, how many fine sights I have missed,
How many curtains have risen without me
And fallen too. How many of my friends
I have not met even once in my life,
How many city skylines
Could have drawn tears from my eyes,
I who know only the one city
And by touch, in my sleep, I could find it . . .
And how many poems I have not written,
Whose secret chorus swirls around my head
And possibly one day
Will stifle me . . .
I know the beginnings and the ends of things,
And life after the end, and something
It isn't necessary to remember now.
And another woman has usurped
The place that ought to have been mine,
And bears my rightful name,
Leaving me a nickname, with which I've done,
I like to think, all that was possible.
But I, alas, won't lie in my own grave.

But sometimes a madcap air in spring,
Or a combination of words in a chance book,

Or somebody's smile, suddenly
Draws me into that non-existent life.
In such a year would such have taken place,
Something else in another: travelling, seeing,
Thinking, remembering, entering a new love
Like entering a mirror, with a dull sense
Of treason, and a wrinkle that only yesterday
Was absent . . .
But if, from that life, I could step aside,
And see my life such as it is, today,
Then at last I'd know what envy means . . .

Leningrad, 1944

The Sixth

There are three epochs in the memory,
And only yesterday, it seems, the first
Occurred. The soul is underneath their blessed
Vault, and the body is basking in their shadow.
Laughter has not died down, and tears are streaming,
A stain of ink is unwiped on the table,
And a kiss is like a seal upon the heart,
Matchless, unforgettable, goodbye . . .
But this one doesn't last long . . . Already
The firmament is not overhead, and somewhere
In a dull suburb is an empty house,
Cold in winter and in summer hot,
Where spiders live and dust lies everywhere,
Letters that were like flames have burnt to ash,
Portraits have been changing stealthily,
And people come to it as to a grave,
And, returning home, they wash their hands
And brush a quick tear from tired lids, heavily
Sighing. But the clock ticks, one spring
Becomes another, the sky turns pink,
Cities change their names, witnesses die,

There is no-one to cry with, no-one to remember
With. And the shades slowly pass from us,
Those shades whom we no longer call upon
And whose return would be terrible to us.
And, once awake, we find we have forgotten
Even the road that led to the lonely house,
And, choked with shame and anger, we run to it,
But everything (as in a dream) is different:
People, things, walls, and no-one knows us—we're
Strangers. We got to the wrong place . . . Oh God!
And now we face the bitterest of all moments:
We realize that we could not contain
This past within the frontiers of our life,
And it has become almost as foreign to us
As to our neighbour in the next apartment.
And that we would not recognize
Those who have died; and those whom God parted
From us, got on splendidly without us—
Even better . . .

1953

Seaside Sonnet

Everything here will outlive me,
Even the houses of the stare
And this air I breathe, the spring air,
Ending its flight across the sea.

Unearthly invincibility . . .
The voice of eternity is calling,
And the light moon's light is falling
Over the blossoming cherry-tree.

It doesn't seem a difficult road,
White, in the chalice of emerald,
Where it's leading I won't say . . .

There between the trunks, a streak
Of light reminds one of the walk
By the pond at Tsarskoye.

1958, Komarovo

Fragment

And it seemed to me that there were fires
Flying till dawn without number,
And I never found out things—those
Strange eyes of his—what colour?

Everything trembling and singing and
Were you my enemy or my friend,
Winter was it or summer?

1959

Summer Garden

I want to visit the roses
In that lonely
Park where the statues remember me young
And I remember them under the water
Of the Neva. In the fragrant quiet
Between the limes of Tsarskoye I hear
A creak of masts. And the swan swims
Still, admiring its lovely
Double. And a hundred thousand steps,
Friend and enemy, enemy and friend,
Sleep. Endless is the procession of shades
Between granite vase and palace door.
There my white nights
Whisper of someone's discreet exalted

Love. And everything is mother-
Of-pearl and jasper,
But the light's source is a secret.

1959, July, Leningrad

In black memory you'll find, fumbling,
A glove to the elbow that unlocks
A Petersburg night. And a crumbling
Air of sweetness in the murky box.
A wind from the gulf. And there, between
The lines of a stormy page,
Blok, smiling scornfully, holds the scene,
The tragic tenor of the age.

Could Beatrice write with Dante's passion,
Or Laura have glorified love's pain?
Women poets – I set the fashion . . .
Lord, how to shut them up again!

1960

Death of a Poet

The unrepeatable voice won't speak again,
Died yesterday and quit us, the talker with groves.
He has turned into the life-giving ear of grain
Or into the gentlest rain of which he sang.
And all the flowers that grow only in this world
Came into bloom to meet his death.
And straightway it's grown quiet on the planet
That bears a name so modest . . . Earth.

1960

The Death of Sophocles

Then the king learnt that Sophocles was dead

(Legend)

To Sophocles' house that night an eagle flew down
    from the sky,
And sombrely rang from the garden the cicadas' choir.
At that hour the genius was passing into immortality,
Skirting, at the walls of his native town, the night-fires
Of the enemy. And this was when the king had a
    strange dream:
Dionysus himself ordered the raising of the siege,
That no noise disturb the Athenians in burying him
With fitting ceremony and with elegies.

1961

Alexander at Thebes

Surely the young king must have been blind to pity
As he spoke the order: 'Destroy Thebes utterly.'
The old general gazed, and knew this place to be
No better than he remembered it, a haughty city.

Put it all to the fire! There were wonders—gate
And tower and temple—everywhere the king searched,
But suddenly his face brightened with a thought:
'Be sure that the house of the Poet is not touched.'

Leningrad, 1961, October

Native Soil

*There's
Nobody simpler than us, or with
More pride, or fewer tears.*
(1922)

Our hearts don't wear it as an amulet,
It doesn't sob beneath the poet's hand,
Nor irritate the wounds we can't forget
In our bitter sleep. It's not the Promised Land.
Our souls don't calculate its worth
As a commodity to be sold and bought;
Sick, and poor, and silent on this earth,
Often we don't give it a thought.
       Yes, for us it's the dirt on our galoshes,
       Yes, for us it's the grit between our teeth.
       Dust, and we grind and crumble and crush it,
       The gentle and unimplicated earth.
But we'll lie in it, become its weeds and flowers,
So unembarrassedly we call it—ours.

1961, Leningrad

There are Four of Us

O Muse of Weeping. . . . .
M. Tsvetaeva

I have turned aside from everything,
From the whole earthly store.
The spirit and guardian of this place
Is an old tree-stump in water.

We are brief guests of the earth, as it were,
And life is a habit we put on.
On paths of air I seem to overhear
Two friendly voices, talking in turn.

Did I say two? . . . There
By the east wall's tangle of raspberry,
Is a branch of elder, dark and fresh.
Why! it's a letter from Marina.

November 1961 (in delirium)

If all who have begged help
From me in this world,
All the holy innocents,
Broken wives, and cripples,
The imprisoned, the suicidal—
If they had sent me one kopeck
I should have become 'richer
Than all Egypt' . . .
But they did not send me kopecks,
Instead they shared with me their strength,
And so nothing in the world
Is stronger than I,
And I can bear anything, even this.

1961

Last Rose

Bowing to the ground with Morozova,
Dancing with the head of a lover,
Flying from Dido's pyre in smoke
To burn with Joan at the stake—

Lord! can't you see I'm weary
Of this rising and dying and living.
Take it all, but once more bring me close
To sense the freshness of this crimson rose.

Komarovo, 1962

It is no wonder that with no happy voice
My still unruly verse speaks now and then
And that I grieve. Already past Phlegethon
Three quarters of my readers have descended.

And you, my friends! So few of you remain
That you are dearer daily. I rejoice
In you. How short the road has become,
That once appeared the longest road of all.

(1964)

What's war? What's plague? We know that they
    will pass,
Judgement is passed, we see an end to them.
But which of us can cope with this fear, this—
The terror that is named the flight of time?

In Memory of V. C. Sreznevskaya

Impossible almost, for you were always here:
In the shade of blessed limes, in hospitals and
    blockades,
In the prison-cell, and where there were evil birds,
Lush grasses, and terrifying water.
How everything has changed, but you were always here,
And it seems to me that I have lost half my soul,
The half you were—in which I knew the reason why
Something important happened. Now I've forgotten . . .
But your clear voice is calling and it asks me not
To grieve, but wait for death as for a miracle.
What can I do! I'll try.

Komarovo, 9 September 1964

You will hear thunder and remember me,
And think: she wanted storms. The rim
Of the sky will be the colour of hard crimson,
And your heart, as it was then, will be on fire.

That day in Moscow, it will all come true,
When, for the last time, I take my leave,
And hasten to the heights that I have longed for,
Leaving my shadow still to be with you.

1961–1963

Requiem

No, not under a foreign heavenly-cope, and
Not canopied by foreign wings—
I was with my people in those hours,
There where, unhappily, my people were.

In the fearful years of the Yezhov terror I spent seventeen months in prison queues in Leningrad. One day somebody 'identified' me. Beside me, in the queue, there was a woman with blue lips. She had, of course, never heard of me; but she suddenly came out of that trance so common to us all and whispered in my ear (everybody spoke in whispers there): 'Can you describe this?' And I said: 'Yes, I can.' And then something like the shadow of a smile crossed what had once been her face.

1 April 1957, Leningrad

Dedication

The mountains bow before this anguish,
The great river does not flow.
In mortal sadness the convicts languish;
The bolts stay frozen. There's someone who
Still feels the sunset's glow,
Someone who can still distinguish
Day from night, for whom the fresh
Wind blows. But we don't know it, we're obsessive,
We only hear the tramp of boots, abrasive
Keys scraping against our flesh.
Rising as though for early mass,
Through the capital of beasts we'd thread.
Met, more breathless than the dead,
Mistier Neva, lower sun. Ahead,
Hope was still singing, endlessly evasive.
The sentence! and now at last tears flood.
She'd thought the months before were loneliness!
She's thrown down like a rock.
The heart gives up its blood.
Yet goes . . . swaying . . . she can still walk.
My friends of those two years I stood
In hell—oh all my chance friends lost
Beyond the circle of the moon, I cry
Into the blizzards of the permafrost:
Goodbye. Goodbye.

Prologue

In those years only the dead smiled,
Glad to be at rest:
And Leningrad city swayed like
A needless appendix to its prisons.
It was then that the railway-yards
Were asylums of the mad;
Short were the locomotives'
Farewell songs.
Stars of death stood
Above us, and innocent Russia
Writhed under bloodstained boots, and
Under the tyres of Black Marias.

I

They took you away at daybreak. Half wak-
ing, as though at a wake, I followed.
In the dark chamber children were crying,
In the image-case, candlelight guttered.
At your lips, the chill of an ikon,
A deathly sweat at your brow.
I shall go creep to our wailing wall,
Crawl to the Kremlin towers.

Gently flows the gentle Don,
Yellow moonlight leaps the sill,

Leaps the sill and stops aston-
ished as it sees the shade

Of a woman lying ill,
Of a woman stretched alone.

Son in irons and husband clay.
Pray. Pray.

No, it is not I, it is someone else who is suffering.
I could not have borne it. And this thing which has
    happened,
Let them cover it with black cloths,
And take away the lanterns . . .
                        Night.

Someone should have shown you—little jester,
Little teaser, blue-veined charm-
er, laughing-eyed, lionised, sylvan-princessly
Sinner—to what point you would come:
How, the three hundredth in a queue,
You'd stand at the prison gate
And with your hot tears
Burn through the New-Year ice.
How many lives are ending there! Yet it's
Mute, even the prison-poplar's
Tongue's in its cheek as it's swaying.

5

For seventeen months I've called you
To come home, I've pleaded
—O my son, my terror!—grovelled
At the hangman's feet.
All is confused eternally—
So much, I can't say who's
Man, who's beast any more, nor even
How long till execution.
Simply the flowers of dust,
Censers ringing, tracks from a far
Settlement to nowhere's ice.
And everywhere the glad
Eye of a huge star's
Still tightening vice.

6

Lightly the weeks are flying,
What has happened, I can't take in.
Just as, my dearest, the white
Nights first watched you in prison,
So they again gaze down
With their warm aquiline eyes and
Of your cross transcendent
And of death I hear them speak.

7

The Sentence

Then fell the word of stone on
My still existing, still heaving breast.
Never mind, I was not unprepared, and
Shall manage to adjust to it somehow.

Thank God, I've many things to do today—I
Need to kill and kill again
My memory, turn my heart to stone, as
Well as practise skills gone rusty, such

As to live, for instance . . . Then there's always
Summer, calling out my Black Sea dress!
Yes, long ago I knew this day:
This radiant day, and this empty house.

8

To Death

You will come in any case, so why not now?
Life is very hard: I'm waiting for you.
I have turned off the lights and thrown the door wide open
For you, so simple and so marvellous.
Take on any form you like.
Why not burst in like a poisoned shell,
Or steal in like a bandit with his knuckleduster,
Or like a typhus-germ?
Or like a fairy-tale of your own invention—
Stolen from you and loathsomely repeated,
Where I can see, behind you in the doorway,
The police-cap and the white-faced concierge?
I don't care how. The Yenisei is swirling,
The Pole Star glittering. And eyes
I love are closing on the final horror.

9

Already madness trails its wing
Decisively across my mind;
I drink its fiery wine and sink
Into the valley of the blind.

I yield to it the victory:
There is no time, there is no room
Except to sue for peace with my
—However strange—delirium.

I fall upon my knees, I pray
For mercy. It makes no concession.
Clearly I must take away
With me not one of my possessions—

Not the stone face, hollow blanks
Of eyes, my son's, through pain's exquisite
Chisel; not the dead's closed ranks
In the hour of prison visits;

Not the dear coolness of his hands;
Nor, dimmed in distance's elision,
Like limetrees' shady turbulence,
His parting words of consolation.

10

Crucifixion

*'Mother, do not weep for Me,
who am in the grave.'*

I

Angelic choirs the unequalled hour exalted,
And heaven disintegrated into flame.
Unto the Father: 'Why hast Thou forsaken . . .!'
But to the Mother: 'Do not weep for me . . .'

II

Magdalina beat her breast and wept, while
The loved disciple seemed hammered out of stone.
But, for the Mother, where she stood in silence,—
No one as much as dared to look that way.

Epilogue

I

There I learned how faces fall apart,
How fear looks out from under the eyelids,
How deep are the hieroglyphics
Cut by suffering on people's cheeks.
There I learned how silver can inherit
The black, the ash-blond, overnight,
The smiles that faded from the poor in spirit,
Terror's dry coughing sound.
And I pray not only for myself,
But also for all those who stood there
In bitter cold, or in the July heat,
Under that red blind prison-wall.

II

Again the hands of the clock are nearing
The unforgettable hour. I see, hear, touch

All of you: the cripple they had to support
Painfully to the end of the line; the moribund;

And the girl who would shake her beautiful head and
Say: 'I come here as if it were home.'

I should like to call you all by name,
But they have lost the lists. . . .

I have woven for them a great shroud
Out of the poor words I overheard them speak.

I remember them always and everywhere,
And if they shut my tormented mouth,

Through which a hundred million of my people cry,
Let them remember me also. . . .

And if ever in this country they should want
To build me a monument

I consent to that honour,
But only on condition that they

Erect it not on the sea-shore where I was born:
My last links there were broken long ago,

Nor by the stump in the Royal Gardens,
Where an inconsolable young shade is seeking me,

But here, where I stood for three hundred hours
And where they never, never opened the doors for me.

Lest in blessed death I should forget
The grinding scream of the Black Marias,

The hideous clanging gate, the old
Woman wailing like a wounded beast.

And may the melting snow drop like tears
From my motionless bronze eyelids,

And the prison pigeons coo above me
And the ships sail slowly down the Neva.

Poem without a Hero

a triptych

1940 – 1962

Leningrad – Tashkent – Moscow

Di rider finirai
Pria dell'aurora

Don Giovanni

Foreword

Deus conservat omnia

motto on the coat of arms of the
House on the Fontanka

Some are no more, others are distant . . .

The poem first came to me, in the House on the Fontanka, on the night of 27 December 1940, though I had been forewarned by a brief fragment the previous autumn. I did not summon it, I did not even expect it, on that cold and dark day of my last winter in Leningrad.

That night I wrote '1913' and a dedication. Early in January I wrote, almost to my surprise, 'Obverse'; and later, in Tashkent, 'Epilogue', which was to become part three, together with some important additions to the first two parts. I continued to work on the poem after my return to Leningrad on 1 June 1944.

I frequently hear of certain absurd interpretations of *Poem without a Hero*. And I have been advised to make it clearer. This I decline to do. It contains no third, seventh, or twenty-ninth thoughts. I shall neither explain nor change anything. What is written is written.

I dedicate the poem to the memory of its first audience—my friends and fellow citizens who perished in Leningrad during the siege. Their voices I hear, and I remember them, when I read my poem aloud, and for me this secret chorus has become a permanent justification of the work.

Dedicatory Poems

I

in memory of Vs.K.

. . . .
Having run out of paper,
I am writing on your rough draft.
And a word which is not mine
Occasionally shows through
Only to melt, trustingly, without reproach,
As snowflakes, once, on my hand.
And the dark eyclashes of Antinoüs
Lifted suddenly—and the green smoke
And our native breeze gently blew . . .   10
Isn't it the sea?
                No, it's only graveyard
Pine-needles, and in a boiling of foam,
Still closer, closer . . .
                Marche funèbre . . .
                                Chopin . . .

2

to O.A.G-S.

Is it you, my blundering Psyche,
Waving your black-and-white fan,
Who lean over me?
Do you wish to tell me in secret   20

You've already crossed the Lethe
And are breathing another spring?
You needn't tell me, I can hear it:
A warm downpour is pressing on the roof,
I hear whispering in the ivy.
Someone small has made up his mind to live,
Has turned green—tomorrow, fluffed up,
Will try to strut in a new cloak.
I sleep—
She alone leans over me, 30
She whom people call spring
I call loneliness.
I sleep— I dream
Of our youth.
That cup which passed him by
I'll give you, if you wish, as a keepsake:
Like a pure flame in clay,
Like a snowdrop in a grave.

3

I have frozen enough with terror,
Better summon up a Bach chaconne, 40
And behind it will come a man
Who won't become my husband, yet together
We shall deserve such things
That the twentieth century will stand agape.
He will be late, this foggy night,
Coming to drink the new year wine
In the palace on the Fontanka.
And he will remember the epiphany,
Maple at the window, wedding candles,
A poem's deathly flight . . . 50
But he will bring me, not a ring,
The first lilac nor that other sweetness, prayer—
Doom is the gift he'll bring.

RAISED HIGH, THE NINETEEN-FORTIETH YEAR
IS A TOWER. I CAN SEE ALL.
I'M SAYING GOODBYE, AS IT WERE,
TO WHAT I HAVE LONG ABANDONED;
CROSSING MYSELF, AND DESCENDING
UNDER THE DARK VAULTS OF BURIAL.

—Leningrad under siege
25 August 1941

PART ONE

The Year Nineteen Thirteen

I

New Year's Eve. The House on the Fontanka. Instead of her expected guest, the author is visited by shadows from the year 1913, disguised as mummers. A white hall of mirrors. Lyrical digression: 'A visitor from the future'. Masquerade. A poet. A ghost.

I have lit my sacred candles,   60
　　One by one, and with your absent
　　　　Companionship I hallow
　　　　　　The coming forty-first year.
But . . .
　　　　God grant us his power!
　　In crystal the flame is drowning,
　　　　'And the wine, like poison, burns.'
Malicious conversations,
　　The resurrection of ravings,
　　　　Though the hour has not yet struck . . .   70
No measure in my terror,
　　I'm a shadow on the threshold
　　　　Defending my last peace.
I listen to the insistent
　　Doorbell, cold mist on
　　　　My skin. I'm stone. Ice. Fire . . .

I half-turn, as if stricken
   By memory, as if my distant
      Voice is saying, 'You're wrong:
This isn't the Doge's Palace.   80
   It's next door.   But your masks and
      Cloaks, your sceptres and your crowns,
Leave them in the hall.   Welcome!
   Animate the New Year revel:
      It's you I celebrate.'
Here's Faust—and here's Don Juan,
   John the Baptist, Dapertutto,
      Dorian Gray; and here's the frugal
         Most northerly of the satyrs,
            Glahn. They whisper their Dianas   90
               With phrases learnt by rote.
                  Here's somebody trailing Pan—a
                     Faun with the legs of a goat.
And for them the walls have widened,
   Lights cascading, sirens whining,
      A cupola is bursting the roof.
Publish the whole scandal!
   What to me are Hamlet's garters!
      The whirlwind of Salome's dancing,
         The tread of the Iron Masker!   100
            I am more iron than they . . .
Whose turn is it now to blench with
   Fear, back away, surrender,
      Ask mercy for an ancient sin? . . .
Clearly it's
            it's me they seek—crazy!
   I've denied them, and my table
      Is set for someone else.
A tail under a dress-suit . . .
   How lame yet elegant . . .   110
                     However . . .
   The Prince of Darkness: whoever
      Would dare to bring him here?
Mask, or skull, or face, his
   Expression of malice and ache I

Doubt even Goya could paint.
The suavest and the sickest,
　　Compared with whom what sinner
　　　Is not incarnate grace?
Enough! Join in the dancing!　　　　　　120
　　But by what necromancy
　　　Am I living and they dead?
In the morning I shall waken,
　　Nobody here to blame me,
　　　Straight into my face the
　　　　Blue will laugh through the pane.
But now I'm frightened. I have
　　Got to present myself, smile at
　　　Them all and fall silent,
　　　　Hugging my lace shawl.　　　　130
She who was I, in her black agate
　　Necklace—till the valley of God's anger
　　　Bring us together, I'd rather
　　　　She kept out of my way . . .
Are the last days close upon us?
　　Your lessons I have forgotten,
　　　Sloganwriters, false prophets,
　　　　You haven't forgotten me.
As in the past the future is maturing,
　　So the past is rotting in the future—　　140
　　　A terrible carnival of dead leaves.

A sound of steps of those not here
Over the gleaming parquet. Blue
Cigar-smoke.   All the mirrors show one who
Would not gain entry if he should appear.
No better, no worse, than others—but frigid
Lethe's not touched him, and his hand is warm.
Guest from the future, will he really come,
Taking the left turn across the bridge?

From childhood I have feared mummers.　　150
　　It always seemed to me that someone,
　　　A kind of extra shade

'Without face or name', has slipped in
  Among them . . .
                Shall we begin by
  Calling the roll on this
Triumphal New Year's Day! But
  Don't expect my midnight Tale of
    Hoffmann to be laid bare . . .
                    Wait! You!   160
Your name's not here, I don't see it
  Among the Magi, Cagliostros, Messalinas,
    You come in the motley stripes
Of a milepost, that brilliant mask the
  Snow wears. You . . . old as the Mamre
    Oak, interlocutor of the moon.
Your feigned groans, they cannot
  Fool us. You write iron commandments;
    Solon, Lycurgus, Hammurabi,
      Should sit down at your feet.   170
His extraordinary nature
  Doesn't wait for gout and fame to
    Arrive in a heat and raise him
      To a pompous jubilee chair.
But over the flowering heather
  And over wildernesses
    He bears his triumph. And
He's not even guilty of bending
  Any law . . .
              Besides, in general,   180
  Poets are blind to sin,
They must dance before the Ark of
  The Covenant, or perish! . . .
                But that's apparent
  In their verses, I'll hold my peace.
We only dream it's cock-crow. The
  Neva is billowing with smoke. Night
    Is fathomless. The sabbat goes on
      And on in Petersburg . . .
In narrow windows the stars are   190
  Muffled in shrouds of disaster

But the liquid tongues of the maskers
      Run lightly through their shames.
A shout:
            'The hero's on stage!'   Ah
   Yes, here he comes, displacing
      The tall one without fail and
      Of holy vengeance he sings.
—But why have you all fled, as
   Though to a communal wedding,   200
      Leaving me in the gloom
Face to face with a frame's blackness
   Out of which stares that hour
      Which became most bitter drama
      Never sufficiently wept.

> *It floods me not all at once*
> *But like a musical phrase.*
> *I hear a whisper: 'Goodbye!*
> *I shall leave you behind,*
> *But you will be my widow,*   210
> *You, my dove, my sun, my sister!'*
> *On the landing, two locked shadows . . .*
> *Then, down the broad stairs,*
> *A scream: 'Don't do it!' Far off*
> *A pure voice:*
> *   'I am ready for death.'*

The torches go out, the ceiling lowers. The white hall
of mirrors becomes the author's room. Words from the
darkness:

Clearly, there's no death.   Saying
   What's clear to all is banal.
      I'd like it explained to me.
                        That knock!   220
I thought they were all within.   Is
   This the guest from behind the mirror,
      The shape that flitted past the pane?

Is the new moon playing a joke, or
   —Between the cupboard and the stove—is
      Somebody standing again?
Pale forehead, open lids, this
   Means that gravestones are brittle,
      That granite is softer than wax . . .
Crazy, crazy, crazy! From such crazes   230
   I shall soon be turning grey or change to
      Something else. Why
Are you beckoning me near?

      For one moment of peace here
      I would give up the grave's peace.

Across the Landing

(Intermezzo)

'Surely you've heard, it's all over . . .
   You're a baby, Signor Casanova . . .'
      'See you at Isaac's at six . . .'
'We'll find you somehow in the fog,
   We've promised to call at the Dog . . .'   240
      'How about you?'—
                  'God knows!'
Don Quixotes, Sancho Panzas,
   Alas, Sodom's celebrants are
      Stumbling, death's wine flows.
Foam-borne Aphrodites risen,
   Helens shivering in the mirror,
      And the age of dementia moves
Nearer. From Fontanka's grotto,
   Weary of his burning-glass, love   250
      Cools and through a horn-gate passes,
        And someone ginger and shaggy
           Leads out the goat-footed nymph.

Brightest star of the scene, though
   Her mask prevents her from seeing,
      Hearing, praying, cursing, breathing,
         Is the head of Madame de Lamballe.
But you, our beauty, our joker,
   Spinning to the whim of the goatking,
      Your lisp is tender and soulful: 260
'Que me veut mon Prince Carnaval?'

Simultaneously in the depths of the hall, stage, hell—or
the summit of Goethe's Brocken—*she* appears (or
perhaps it is her shadow):

Horns in her pale curls, shoes are
   Beating a rhythm of hoofbeats,
      Drunk with the oceanic dance—
As if from a figured vase she
   Goes whirling towards the azure
      Wave, in naked elegance
And earrings ringing like sleighbells.
   And you, in helmet and greatcoat,
      Behind, who bare-faced came here,   270
      You, Ivanushka of the fable,
         What wearies you today?
So much bitterness in each word,
   Over your love so black a cloud,
      And why does that streak of blood
         Rip the petal of your cheek?

The heroine's bedroom. A wax candle is burning. Over the bed are three portraits of the mistress of the house in various roles. On the right, the goatlegged nymph; in the centre, the blunderer; on the left a portrait in shadows. Some might think it Columbine; others, Donna Anna from 'The Steps of the Commendatore'. Outside the mansard window piccaninnies are playing snowballs. A blizzard rages. New Year's Night. The blunderer comes alive, glides from the portrait, and she hears a voice reading aloud:

My dove, throw wide your satin
  Cloak! And don't be angry
    That I have touched this chalice:
      I condemn myself, not you.   280
It is time to settle old scores
  —Look, in the grainy storm
    Meyerhold's blackamoors
      Are romping about again.
And round us is Peter's creation
  That flayed the hide of the nation
    (As the nation expressed it then).
In manes, harnesses, meal-carts,
  In the variegated tea-rose,
    And under raven-wing clouds.   290
With the image of a smile, our
  Mariinsky prima, our dying
    Ineffable swan is flying,
      And the late snob enters loud.
Orchestral sounds from that other
  World, something's shadow flashed somewhere
    —Has the dawn already fluttered
      A premonition along the rows?
And again our glory and wonder,
  The voice like an echo of thunder,   300
    Chaliapin, throws

All the heart's electric,
   Riding over the land that bred him,
      All its unridable ways.
Branches in the blue-white snow . . .
   Who walks the twelve colleges' corridor now
      Will dream that he is walking through
         An echo of all that's happened, so
            Endless it is, hollow and straight.
Absurdly close, the finale: 310
   From behind screens, the mask of
      Petrushka, coachmen round fires dance, the
         Palace flies a yellow-black flag.
Everything's here that we need.   The
   Fifth and final act breathes from
      The Summer Garden . . . Tsushima's
         Hell is here.   —A drunken sailor sings.
Fly, shadows! —your sleigh-runners
   A-jingle, the she-goat's sleigh-rug a-
      Trail! —He's here alone.   320
Sharp shadow on the wall, face of
   Mephistophilis or Gabriel—
      My lady, your paladin?
Demon with the smile of Tamara,
   What are the secrets of charm in
      That terrible smoky face?
Flesh dragged towards spirit as a rock
   Quarried for the sculptor's block—
      All mystery, all outer space.
He, was it, through the packed hall,   330
   Sent you (or was it a dream?) a champagne-
      Glass containing a black rose?
With dead heart, dead expression,
   He met the commendatore, stepping
      Heavily into the cursed house.
He, was it, who first mentioned
   How you were both in a dimension
      Outside the laws of space and time—
There, in what polar crystals,
   And in what amber glister,   340

At the Lethe's—at the Neva's—mouth.
Out of the portrait you ran,
  And until the rising sun
    The frame will wait on the wall.
So dance now—dance, unescorted.
  If you crave a fatal chorus
    I consent to the role.

> *Scarlet spots on your cheeks;*
> *You'd better return to the canvas.*
> *But tonight is the kind of night*   350
> *When accounts must be settled . . .*
> *Yet this intoxicating drowsiness*
> *Is harder to fight than death.*

From nowhere you came to Russia,
  O my blond-haired wonder,
    Our second decade's columbine:
Why do you gaze so sharply and sadly,
  Petersburg doll and actress,
    You, my double, my twin.
Yes, write that title below your   360
  Others.   Companion of poets,
    I inherited one of your crowns.
In the divinely musical metre
  Of Leningrad's keen wind,
    In the shade of a protected cedar,
      I see a dance of courtly bones.
The wedding candles gutter,
  Veiled shoulders are kissed, a thunder
    Of church commands: 'Dove, alight!'
A meeting in a Maltese chapel,   370
  Parma violets heaped in April
    Like a curse within your heart.
Vision of the golden age, or
  A black crime in the chaos
    Of our dreadful former years?

Tell me this at least:
            did you
  Really, at some moment, live, your
    Tiny feet gliding on air
      While others trod the paved squares?   380
Your house like a carnival wagon,
  Peeling cupids standing
    At the alter of Venus on guard.
Your singing birds free as larks, you
  Furnished your bedroom like an arbour,
    —Who'd recognise this rustic maid?
Hidden in the walls are spiral
  Staircases; saints on the sky-blue
    Walls . . . Stolen goods . . . but all in bloom
Like the Spring of Botticelli,   390
  You received your friends in
    Bed, and your languishing dragoon
Pierrot who wore the smile of
  An evening sacrifice, that
    Most religious of your admirers—
      You were a magnet to his steel.
He's white, the tears are flowing,
  He sees you showered with roses,
    And his rival's revered by all.
I cannot see your husband.   400
  The fortress clock has struck.   I
    Am pressed against the glass—frost.
I don't chalk crosses on houses,—
  Step bravely to this encounter—
    Long ago your horoscope was cast.

3

> *In Petersburg we'll gather again,*
> *Around the grave where we buried the sun.*

> Mandelstam

Petersburg, 1913. Lyrical interlude: last recollection in Tsarskoye Selo. A wind, reminiscent or prophetic, mutters:

Bonfires cooked the geese of Christmas,
  Carriages toppled from bridges,
    The whole funereal city swam
On a blind assignation
  Down the Neva or against it   410
    —Only away, away from its graves.
All its arches were throbbing black molars,
  The Summer Garden's vane was crowing
    Thinly, a bright moon turned a colder
      Silver over the silver age.
Since, along all roads and
  Towards all thresholds, slowly
    A shadow advanced, the wind
Was ripping posters off the
  Walls, smoke whirled in cossack   420
    Dances on the roofs,
Lilac breathed a graveyard smell, and
  The city, demented and dostoyevsky,
    Wrapped itself in its fog.
Peter, old genius, old assassin,
  Stared again out of blankness,
    Beat an execution drum . . .
And always, something not thunder
  Under the profligate frost, a rumble
    Of war before it began.   430

But then it was heard so faintly
   It scarcely touched the ear, as flakes to
      The Neva's drifts it drowned.
As though, in night's terrible mirror
   Man, raving, denied his image
      And tried to disappear,—
While along the embankment of history,
   Not the calendar—the existing
      Twentieth century drew near.

> *And now to go home, swiftly,*   440
> *Through the Cameron gallery,*
> *To the icy mysterious park,*
> *Where the waterfalls are silent,*
> *Where I must make all nine glad*
> *As once I was dear to you.*
> *Beyond the park, beyond the island,*
> *Can it be that our eyes won't*
> *Meet with their clear former gaze?*
> *Won't you really ever whisper*
> *To me again that word which*   450
>   *kills*
>   *death*
>   *And is my life's one clue?*

4

The corner of Mars Field. A house built early in the
nineteenth century by the brothers Adamini. In the
bombing of 1942 it will suffer a direct hit. A bonfire
flames high. The sound of bells pealing from the Church
of the Saviour on the Blood. In the square through a
snowstorm, the apparition of a court ball. Silence itself
speaks, in the lulls between these sounds:

Who stands stiff at the dimmed windows, on his
    Heart that 'blonde curl',
        Total darkness before his eyes?
'Help me!   It's not too late!   I
    Have never seen you, night, so strange, so
        Frosty!'   The wind, deranged,
Laden with cargoes of salt . . . It's   460
    Not the Champs de Mars but the Baltic.
        Invisible hooves ring . . .
His agitation cannot be sounded
    Whose whole life is running aground and
        Whose only prayer's for a boundless
            Forgetting and forgotten sleep.
He, roaming beyond midnight under
    Those corner windows; dully
        A street light points at him.
His wait is rewarded . . . An elegant masker   470
    On the road back from Damascus
        Is coming home . . . she's not alone.
Someone with her without face or
    Name . . . Unappeasable separation
        He saw through the oblique
Bonfire flames.   Then houses fell and
    Produced a sobbing echo:
        'I shall leave you behind,
O my dove, my sun, my sister,
    But you will be my widow,   480
        And now . . . Goodbye.   It's time.'

The landing's drugged with perfume,
  And a cadet dragoon with verses
    And senseless death in his breast
Will ring, if his courage suffices,
  That he may waste one final
    Moment glorifying you.
                              Behold:
Not on the cursed marshes of Mazur,
  Not on Carpathia's azure   490
    Peaks— in your own house!
      Blocking the door! . . .

      Et te conservet Deus.

        So many ways for a poet to die,
        Stupid child, to choose this one,—
        Couldn't endure the first hurt,
        Ignorant on what threshold
        He stood, the opening view
        Of what road.

And it was I, your ancient   500
  Conscience, found the burnt pages
    Of a story, in his home,
      Placed on the edge of a sill
        The dead boy's will
          And on tiptoe left the room.

ALL IS IN ORDER: THE POEM LIES
AND, AS IS NATURAL TO IT, RESTS.
BUT WHAT IF, SUDDENLY, THE THEME ESCAPES

AND HAMMERS ON THE WINDOW WITH ITS
   FISTS,—
ANSWERED BY DISTANT, DREADFUL
   SOUNDS—
A CLICKING IN THE THROAT, A RATTLE,
AND A VISION OF CROSSED HANDS . . .

510

PART TWO

Obverse

My future is in my past

I drink the water of Lethe,
My doctor won't allow me depression

Pushkin

The House on the Fontanka, 5 January 1941. Through the window the ghost of a snow-covered maple. The devilish harlequinade has just rushed by, disturbing the silence of the soundless age, and leaving behind the disorder common to all festive or funeral processions—torch-smoke, scattered flowers on the floor, holy relics forever lost . . . A wind howls in the chimney, and in this howl may be divined snatches of Requiem, deeply and cunningly hidden. Of what appears in the mirrors, it is better not to think.

I

My editor showed displeasure,
   Pleaded sickness, pleaded a deadline,
     Then, restricting his phone,
Grumbled: 'It's got to be simpler!
   You read, and when you've finished
     You still don't know who's in love

II

With whom, who met and why, who
  Lived and who died, who's
    Author and who's hero.   And
Ideologically it's outmoded,
  This carrying-on about a poet
    And a swarm of ghosts.'

520

III

I answered: 'There were three—
  A milepost was the chief,
    Another like the devil was dressed.
Behind them their poems labour
  To help them achieve the ages.
    The third, at twenty, was dead,

530

IV

And I pity him.' And again
  Word fell out over word,
    The music box droned on.
And the clever poison flamed
  Over that bottle-hard
    Angry and corkscrew tongue.

V

I dreamt that I was held to
  Creating a libretto
    For music that flowed evermore.
And a dream—is something substantial,
  The Blue Bird, the soft embalmer,
    The ramparts of Elsinore.

540

VI

And I myself was not glad
  To receive that harlequinade,
    To hear that distant scream.

I kept hoping that like puffs of
   Smoke pine-needles would be gusted
      Past the white hall, through the gloom.

VII

With such an elegant Satan
   —So colourful—this motley ancient   550
      Cagliostro, you can't resist.
It goes against his belief
   To mourn the dead, for grief
      And conscience do not exist.

VIII

Well . . . it doesn't smell of a Roman
   Carnival.   Over the closed domes a
      Melody of cherubim
Trembles.   No-one is hammering on my
   Door, only the stillness watches
      Over stillness, mirror of mirror dreams.   560

IX

And with me is my 'Seventh',
   Mute, half-dead, a
      Puckered grimace its mouth,
That could be the mouth of a tragic
   Mask, but for the black daub,
      The stuffed-in dry earth.

X

  . . . .
    . . . .
      . . . .
And the decades pass: tortures,   570
   Exile, executions—*you're* not
      Surprised that I can't sing.

XI

And especially when our dreams imagine
    All that must still be enacted:
        Death everywhere—our city burnt through . . .
And Tashkent in flower for a wedding . . .
    Very soon the asiatic wind will tell me
        What is eternal and true.

XII

XIII

Shall I be melted to a state hymn?
    I don't want, don't want, a diadem
        From a dead poet's brow.
The time will come for my lyre,
    But Sophocles we need, not Shakespeare.
        Fate is the night-visitor now.

590

XIV

And the theme that came
    Was a crushed chrysanthemum
        On the floor when the coffin has passed.
Between memory and call-to-mind is
    The distance of Luga's ice-fields
        From the land of the satin half-mask.

XV

The devil made me rummage . . .
    Yet how is it, I wonder,
        I am so steeped in guilt?

I of the quiet, simple manner,
  I the 'White Flock' and the 'Plantain' . . .
    How, my friends, excuse my fault?

XVI

If it is so confused it's
  Because I don't hide my confusion.
    As you know, I'm a plagiarist . . .
Anyway, I am indifferent
  To failure . . . box with a triple
    Bottom . . . Time I confessed

XVII

At least to one crime: I write
  In invisible ink, and light
    Breaks only when it's reflected
In a glass.   Since I am bereft
  All others, from this one road left
    I shall not quickly be deflected.

XVIII

If an angel had stooped in its flight
  Home to El Greco's heaven
    To explain to me wordlessly
But with a summer smile
  That more than all the seven
    Deadly sins he was forbidden me.

XIX

Then, if the unknown human
  Stepping out of the future
    Will impudently flash
His eyes and give to the flying
  Shade an armful of wet lilac
    In the hour when this storm has passed.

XX

But the century-old enchantress
   Suddenly woke up, felt like dancing,
      Making merry.   I'm at a loss.
Drops her lace handkerchief, languid   630
   Eyes look up from her stanzas,
      She gestures me across.

XXI

I've drunk of her, every drop,
   Didn't know how to stop
      The black thirst possessing me,
Binding me to her ravings:
   I threatened the Star Chamber,
      And drove her to her natal den—

XXII

To the darkness under Manfred's fir,
   And where Shelley, dead on the shore,   640
      Looked straight up into the sky,
While Byron held the brand, and
   All the world's skylarks shattered
      The dome beneath eternity.

XXIII

But she said in her most clear
   Voice: 'I am not that English muse,
      Not La Belle Dame Sans Merci;
July it was who brought me here,
   Except for the solar, the fabulous,
      I have no ancestry.   650

XXIV

But for all your equivocal glory
   Twenty years in the ditch, I
     Shall still not serve you thus,
But will compensate with a royal
   Kiss your wicked midnight.
     Sit, and feast with us.'

PART THREE

Epilogue

I love you, creation of Peter!

Pushkin: *The Bronze Horseman*

White night of 24 June 1942. The city in ruins. From
the harbour to Smolny it is spread out to the gaze. Here
and there old fires are burning themselves out. In the
Sheremetyev Garden, limes are in flower and a night-
ingale is singing. A window on the third storey has been
blown out, and behind it a black emptiness gapes.
From the direction of Kronstadt heavy guns are audible.
But generally it is quiet. Seven thousand kilometres
away, the author's voice:

To my city

Inside the House on the Fontanka
   Where with a bunch of keys, a lantern,
     The evening lassitude
Begins, with an out-of-place laugh I   660
   Hallooed to a distant echo, shattered
     The unbroken sleep of things;
Where, witness of all in the world,
   At dawn or twilight, an old
     Maple looks into the room

And, foreseeing my absence,
  Stretches out his dried and blackened
    Arm as if to help.
Earth hummed beneath my feet and
  The red planet was streaking   670
    Through my still unbroken roof.
It listened for its own password—that
  Sound that is all around us . . .
    And in Tobruk . . . it is everywhere.
You, not the first nor the last dark
  Auditor of bright madness,
    What vengeance do you prepare for me?
You will only sip, not drain to
  Its depths this bitter taste of
    Our separation.   Understand   680
There is no need to set your
  Hand upon my head.   Put an end to
    Time, let it forever remain
Here like a bookmark in a book at
  The silence of the cuckoo
    In the arson of our woods . . .

> *And behind barbed wire*
> *In the dense taiga's heart*
> *—I don't know in what year*
> *Transformed to a pile of camp-dust, an*   690
> *Anecdote from the terrible fact—*
> *My double goes to interrogation,*
> *With two thugs sent by the Noseless Slut,*
> *And I hear from where I stand*
> *—Isn't that a miracle!—*
> *The sound of my own voice:*
>   *I have paid for you in cash,*
>   *For ten years I've looked*
>   *Neither right nor left,*
>   *Your ill fame at my back . . .*   700

You, the grave I sprang from,
  Dearest, infernal, granite,
    Have paled, have died, lie still.

It's only imagined, our separation,
  Nothing can split us, efface my
    Shadow that's on your walls,
My reflection in your waters,
  Steps in the Hermitage halls, where
    My friend and I once strolled;
And in ancient Volkovo Field,   710
  Where there's no end to weeping
    The still fraternal graves.
All that the First Part said of
  Love, betrayal and passion,
    Free poetry brushes from its wings,
And my city is shrouded but standing . . .
  Heavy are the slabs that
    Press on your sleepless eyes,
Yet I dreamed in flight I heard you
  Chase me, you who stayed to perish   720
    In an iceblink of waters, a glitter of spires.
You did not wait for the beloved
  Deliverers: a round-dance above you
    Of brief white nights.
But the joyful word—home—
  It is a word unknown to
    All now, all look through foreign panes.
In New York, in Tashkent, the
  Bitter air of exile
    Is like a poisoned wine.   730
How admiringly you'd have watched me
  As in the gut of the dolphin
    I saved myself from the shark,
And over forests infested
  Rushed like a witch's spectre
    To the Brocken in the night.
And already the frozen Kama
  Could be seen, and someone stammered
    'Quo Vadis?' and before lips moved,
      Another panorama,   740
        With bridges and tunnels—the hammer
        Of the Urals pounded below.

And under my eyes unravelled
   That road so many had travelled,
      By which they led away my son.
And that road was long—long—long, amidst the
   Solemn and crystal
                    Stillness
      Of Siberia's earth.
From all that to ash is rendered,   750
   Filled with mortal dread yet
      Knowing the calendar
Of vengeance, having wrung her
   Hands, her dry eyes lowered, Russia
      Walked before me towards the east.

Notes

From *Evening* (St Petersburg, 1912)

Akhmatova had married the poet Nikolai Gumilev in 1910. They lived at Tsarskoye Selo, the Tsar's village near St Petersburg, and most of *Evening* was written there. The marriage was strained from the first, and Gumilev left for a long visit to Africa. 'Since many of the poems in *Evening* date from the period of Gumilev's extended absence . . . it is perhaps not surprising that the greater part of the volume is concerned with a woman who is either unloved or has lost her lover.' (Amanda Haight: *Akhmatova, A Poetic Pilgrimage*)

Critics have noted the influence of Art Nouveau in Akhmatova's early poetry, particularly in its mood of languorous refinement, and in the way that essential details are registered with a few subtle strokes. The former she purged from her style; the latter never left her.

Imitation of Annensky Innokenty Annensky was headmaster of the grammar school at Tsarskoye Selo attended by Gumilev. He published little and late in life, but his poetry was a major inspiration to Akhmatova.

From *Rosary* (St Petersburg, 1914)

Immensely popular, *Rosary* had gone into four impressions by 1916. 'Telling *Rosary*' became a fashionable game—one person starting a poem, another finishing it.

'*I have come to take your place, sister . . .*' Akhmatova was fascinated by doubles. In this poem the two sisters seem to represent

133

aspects of herself, one of which must die for the other to grow: a poet's shedding of skin. As in *By the Sea Shore*, there may be a recollection, also, of an event that cast a shadow over her childhood. When Akhmatova was five, her sister Rika, a year younger, died of T.B. Rika was away staying with an aunt at the time, and her death was kept secret from Akhmatova.

'*We're all drunkards here . . .*' The sense of shame and guilt points forward to the great poem of expiation, *Poem without a Hero*, of her late years. There is a sense of play-acting, in what was the calendar, but not yet the real, twentieth century.

The Voice of Memory Olga Glebova-Sudeikina, a famous St Petersburg actress and beauty, was involved in a tangled love-affair which resulted in the suicide of a young cadet officer and poet, Vsevolod Knyazev. Akhmatova, too, was closely involved. *Poem without a Hero* re-creates this pointless tragedy, which is seen as representative of its era, and seeks to expiate it.

'*Blue heaven, but the high . . .*' The subject of this poem is again, presumably, Knyazev.

'*I came to him as a guest . . .*' Akhmatova's attitude to Blok, the great Symbolist poet, was ambivalent. She admired his genius, but distrusted what she saw as a demonic quality in his nature.

By the Sea Shore was written in 1913 and published in the magazine *Apollon* in 1915.

Akhmatova was born on the Black Sea coast, and though her family soon moved to Tsarskoye Selo they returned to the sea each summer. The sea stayed in Akhmatova's blood. *By the Sea Shore* is her most ambitious early exploration of the theme of the twin or double. One twin is pagan, wild, witch-like, dreaming constantly of her ideal love, the prince or tsarevitch; the other is Christian, confined through illness, responsible, and sensitive to another's sorrow. Not only are the twins two sides of Akhmatova's character: the grey-eyed boy and the tsarevitch 'might also be taken as two sides of the character of the man who dominated Akhmatova's adolescence and finally married her: the tsarevitch who came from the sea—the poet, and the grey-eyed boy—the husband' (Amanda Haight). Childhood innocence, in the poem, passes into the knowledge of death.

From *White Flock* (Petrograd, 1917)

Most of the poems of this collection were written at Slepnyovo, in the province of Tver, where Akhmatova's small son, Lev, was being looked after by Gumilev's mother. According to Amanda Haight, much of *White Flock* relates to Akhmatova's friendship with the artist, Boris Anrep.

'*How can you look at the Neva . . .*' In the St Petersburg winters, bonfires were lit in the streets to melt the snow.

From *Plantain* (Petrograd, 1921)

'*Now no-one will be listening to songs . . .*' The last line reflects Akhmatova's determination to stay and bear witness, rather than go into exile as many of her friends were doing in the post-Revolutionary years.

From *Anno Domini* (Petersburg, 1921)

'*They wiped your slate . . .*' Gumilev, from whom Akhmatova had been divorced in 1918, was executed three years later as an alleged counter-revolutionary. Akhmatova appended a false dating, 1914, to avoid an obvious reference to Gumilev.

Bezhetsk When she visited Slepnyovo in December 1921 to be with her son, the nearby ancient town of Bezhetsk brought back tormenting memories of former happy visits with Gumilev.

Lot's Wife The poet's attitude to the wife of Lot may confirm the expressed view of Mayakovsky, and others, that she was a 'pointless, pathetic and comic anachronism'. Or it may confirm her profound compassion and her fidelity to private emotion. Significantly and ironically, Mayakovsky was reading her poetry almost every day in private.

From *Reed*

Originally entitled *Willow*, *Reed* appeared as a section of *From Six Books* (Leningrad, 1940). It contains a part of the fruit of sixteen years of almost total silence. Akhmatova had been one of the first to feel the State's displeasure. Not knowing quite what to do with her, they had given her—in her mid-thirties—an old-age pension: enough to keep her in cigarettes and matches.

The publication of *From Six Books* came as a surprise. A few months later it was declared to have been an error, and withdrawn.

The poems from the era of silence are few in number, compared with earlier years, but carry immense authority. They strengthen and define her position of independence: through identification with Dante and, less centrally, Shakespeare's Cleopatra; through tributes to contemporary writers of like integrity, Mandelstam, Pasternak, Bulgakov, and to the timeless Muse herself; by affirming her oneness with the earthly world (*Willow*) and the divine world (*Way of all the Earth*). *Requiem*, the tragic and beautiful sequence that arose from her son's arrest, imprisonment and exile, was written during the years 1935–1940. It was not written down, only remembered; it still does not appear in the most recent Soviet edition of her work.

Boris Pasternak 'Darya's gorge': the Daryal gorge runs through the Caucasus into Georgia, which Pasternak often visited in the 1930s to see his friends, the poets Paolo Yashvili and Titsian Tabidze. Both died in the purges, a year after this poem was written. A Georgian legend states that Queen Darya would lure travellers to her tower and hurl their bodies into the turbulent river Terek at the bottom of the gorge.

Voronezh Voronezh is a city about three hundred miles south of Moscow, on a tributary of the Don. Peter the Great built a flotilla there. The Field of Kulikovo, where the Tatars were defeated in 1380, is not far away. Mandelstam lived there in exile from 1934 to 1937. Akhmatova visited him in February 1936.

Imitation from the Armenian Under the thin disguise of the title, the poem obviously refers to the arrest of Akhmatova's son.

In Memory of Mikhail Bulgakov Bulgakov, a close friend of the poet, was an outstanding novelist, satirist and playwright. His great novel, *The Master and Margarita*, was completed in the last year of his life, 1940, but not published in the Soviet Union till 1966.

Way of all the Earth 'Kitezh, according to legend, was a city saved by prayer from the advance of the Tatars. Some say it was lifted up to the heavens and its reflection seen on a lake into which the enemy rushed to their death, others that like other legendary cities it sunk deep into the lake where its towers can be seen on days when the water is specially clear. Akhmatova's "Kitezhanka", the woman of Kitezh, is seen hurrying home through the bullets, across the trenches, through the wars filling half the twentieth century . . . This poem is not, however, about escape from life, but one which expresses faith in the most profound sense of the word. Strength here stems from the recognition that the poet has come from God and will one day return to Him, and that she must make her way through time to the place where there will be none.' (Amanda Haight: *Akhmatova, A Poetic Pilgrimage*)

The *Varyag* and the *Koreyetz* were Russian ships that perished heroically against the Japanese fleet in 1904. *Fort Shabrol* was the sarcastic name given to the house on Shabrol Street, Paris, where the anti-Dreyfus conspirators held out against arrest in 1899. These events, and the 'anti-imperial' Boer War, symbolize the dying age. The poem moves back through the beginnings of World War II (*Part 1* of the poem); World War I—Akhmatova last visited the Crimea in 1916 (*Part 2*); the personal events of her 'crisis' year 1913 (3); Petersburg of the first decade (4); the century's turn (5); and the timeless city (6).

Akhmatova regarded this as the most *avant-garde* work she had written. Its energy, compression, symbolism, mixture of the narrative and the lyrical, its gathering-together of past suffering, as well as certain images—Hoffman, mirrors, Tsushima (where the Russian fleet was destroyed in 1905)—all are reminiscent of *Poem without a Hero*, the work which she began in this year, 1940, and which was to continue to possess her almost till the end of her life. For the poet, aged fifty, this year was a climacteric. Her health, never good, was failing badly, she was extremely poor, and had been living mostly on black bread and sugarless tea;

her son had been sentenced to death, reprieved, and sent into exile; the war in Europe seemed to be destroying the culture of which she felt herself a part; official oppression had eased slightly only to clamp down again, thus further endangering her son; she was terrified that she was going mad. Yet *Requiem* was being completed, and other majestic poems were being written and conceived. As a poet, she was at the height of her powers.

From *The Seventh Book*

Like *Reed*, this was never published as a separate volume.

In 1940 Akhmatova's personal suffering did not stop her feeling grief for the fate of Paris and London. This leads to a memory of one of her friends of 1913 (the year celebrated and condemned in *Poem without a Hero*), Salome Andronnikova, who was living in London. Mandelstam, in a famous poem about her, had punned on her name with a reference to drinking through a straw, (in Russian, *solominka* means 'little straw'). The epigraph to *Shade* is taken from a poem by Mandelstam that addresses another emigré, Olga Vaksel, who had committed suicide in Norway.

'*That's how I am . . .*' Flown out of Leningrad under siege, by a strange whim of the authorities, Akhmatova spent the next three years in Tashkent. She regarded this fresh experience with a mixture of joy, delirium—she became seriously ill with typhus—and recognition (see 'It is your lynx eyes, Asia . . .'). Akhmatova draws a parallel between her own condition and the fate of Marina Tsvetaeva. Tsvetaeva, an emigré since 1922, returned to Russia in 1939, to find that her husband, who had preceded her, had been shot, and her daughter arrested. She hanged herself in 1941, an event which greatly affected Akhmatova.

'*The souls of those I love* . . . Though Akhmatova dated this poem, and the next, in the early forties, it is likely that they were written in 1921, the year of Gunilev's death.

Northern Elegies: Akhmatova conceived seven elegies, but some are fragmentary, and the seventh, evidently particularly important to her, appears to be lost altogether. I follow Haight's numbering, which differs from that in the American edition and the most recent Soviet edition, (Leningrad 1976).

(Fifth) Anna Gorenko adopted the name Akhmatova when she was seventeen, from a real or imagined Tatar great-grandmother. She grew to resent not having a 'real' name; Akhmatova, she said, was 'Tatar, backwoods, coming from nowhere, cleaving to every disaster, itself a disaster'. Another allusion in the poem is to her always-muddled marital status as a married/single/homeless/widow woman.

Two years after this poem was written, the age grew harsher. During the war, her poems had been appearing in magazines, and a *Selected Poems* was published in Tashkent. In 1945, to her surprise and joy, her son returned from the front—he had been released from exile to fight in the war. A selection of her work was printed in Moscow in 1946; but it was never published. Stalin, having dealt with the enemy outside, turned again to destroy the 'enemy within', and Akhmatova bore the first virulence of the attack on 'ideologically harmful and apolitical works'. She was expelled from the Writers' Union, shadowed wherever she went, and, worst of all, her son was re-arrested. He was to spend seven more years in a prison camp. Following Stalin's death, Akhmatova's situation improved, and in the last ten years of her life she was able to live more freely, even visiting the West, and her poetry, though still subject to censorship, was published.

Death of a Poet Boris Pasternak.

There are Four of Us The three poets referred to, besides Akhmatova, are Pasternak, Mandelstam, and Tsvetaeva. The title is that used in the first publication of the poem, which was in an American-Russian language publication, *Paths of Air*. In later Soviet editions of her work, the poem is entitled *Komarovo Sketches*. Akhmatova spent much time in her last years at Komarovo, fifty miles from Leningrad on the Karelian isthmus, and she is buried there. The epigraph, '*O Muse of Weeping*', is the first line of a poem to Akhmatova written in 1916.

Last Rose Morozova was a seventeenth-century dissenter who resisted the reformed ritual of the Orthodox Church and was forcibly removed to Siberia. Akhmatova recited this poem to

Robert Frost when the American poet visited the Soviet Union in 1962.

In Memory of V.C. Sreznevskaya Valeriya Sreznevskaya was one of the poet's oldest and closest friends. They had played together as children at Tsarskoye Selo.

Requiem

It was common practice with Akhmatova to subscribe, after a poem, the date, and sometimes place, of its composition. This information is provided below.

Quatrain. 1961.
Foreword. 'The Yezhov terror', or *yezhovshchina*, is the name Russians give to the worst period of the purges (1937–38), when Nikolai Yezhov was the official whom Stalin entrusted with the operation.
Dedication. March 1950.
1. 1935. In her memoir of Mandelstam, Akhmatova mentions that this poem refers to the arrest of her friend, Nikolai Punin, in 1935. He was released before the Yezhov terror began, and was not rearrested.
2. 'Husband clay' refers to Nikolai Gumilev, shot in 1921. In the original Russian, the last two lines have a peasant-like alliterative ferocity and simplicity that has, I think, eluded all translators.
3. This was published in a Moscow literary journal in 1966.
4. The original text mentions the name of the prison—Kresty (Crosses), perhaps with an allusion to its literal meaning.
5. 1939.
6. 1939.
7. 1939. Summer. This was printed, without title, as long ago as 1940, in the Leningrad literary journal *Zvezda*.
8. 19 August 1939, the House on the Fontanka. 'Police cap': the original has the 'blue cap' of the NKVD uniform. The Yenisei is a river in Siberia.
9. 4 May 1940, the House on the Fontanka.
10. 1940–43.

Epilogue. March 1940. 'Motionless bronze eyelids'—like the famous bronze equestrian statue of Peter the Great.

Poem without a Hero

Foreword

The epigraph is from the last stanza of *Eugene Onegin*. Pushkin takes farewell of his poem, and notes that many of his first readers are no longer around—including those hanged and exiled for their part in the Decembrist uprising. The aptness of the allusion needs no underlining.

'Certain absurd interpretations': many of Akhmatova's contemporaries criticised her for attacking the dead or people so far away they could not answer back.

Dedicatory poems

(1) Vs.K.—Vsevolod Knyazev. But the world of masks and doubles may already have started, for certain features of the poem strongly suggested to Nadezhda Mandelstam that the poem was really dedicated to her husband, who died in a Siberian transit-camp in 1938. 'After hearing Akhmatova recite her *Poem* for the first time in Tashkent, I asked to whom the "First Dedication" was addressed. "Whose first draft do you think I can write on?" she replied with some irritation. . . . I have two copies of the *Poem*. In one of them Knyazev's initials stand just above the "First Dedication", but have been crossed out by Akhmatova—she did this in my presence, saying it was a typing error. The other copy does not have his initials at all.' (Nadezhda Mandelstam: *Hope Abandoned*). If, as seems certain from other evidence too, Mandelstam and Knyazev are blurred together in the poem, they would appear to be mirror-reflections rather than doubles: the novice-poet who withdrew from life before the turmoil began, and the major poet who endured it all, to the anonymous mass-grave.

l. 8, 'Antinoüs': the allusion is probably to a favourite of the Emperor Hadrian, a youth of extraordinary beauty who drowned himself in the Nile in AD 130. Carl Proffer says it refers to the Homeric Antinoüs, braggart suitor to Penelope; but this seems less likely.

(2) O.A.G-S: Olga Glebova-Sudeikina. l. 17, 'blundering Psyche': literally Confusion-Psyche, one of her roles, in a play of the same name by Yury Belayev.

(3) A shadowy figure, presumably the 'guest from the future' (see l. 148, and note).

Part One, 1

l. 67, a quotation from Akhmatova's poem 'A New Year's Ballad', published in her collection *Anno Domini* (1921).

ll. 86–93. The masked guests who stream in are playing roles which were well known in the theatrical and literary life of Petersburg in those years. Don Juan recalls Mozart, Byron, Pushkin (*The Stone Guest*), Blok (*The Steps of the Commendatore*), but more immediately refers to Molière's version of the story, which was staged in 1910 by Vsevolod Meyerhold. 'Dapertutto' was Meyerhold's commedia dell'arte pen name. John the Baptist—from Richard Strauss's opera, based on Wilde's *Salome*, and also a ballet by Fokine. Glahn is a character in Knut Hansun's *Pan*. The 'goatlegged nymph' is Sudeikina: late in 1912 she danced a ballet called *The Fauns*. A contemporary photograph shows her in the costume of a faun, with goat's horns.

l. 94, 'the walls have widened': symbolically, to all Russia.

l. 112, 'The Prince of Darkness': Mikhail Kuzmin.

l. 132, 'the valley of God's anger': the Day of Judgment.

ll. 142–49. This passage was inspired by an actual visitor from the West, Isaiah Berlin, who came to see Akhmatova not long after the war. Under the conditions that prevailed, she regarded the visit as providential, almost literally 'from the future'. In reality, the Soviet authorities used it as one of their excuses for the renewed imprisonment of her son and persecution of herself. Max Hayward points out her extreme precision of detail: to reach her apartment in a wing of the old Sheremetyev Palace, it would have been necessary to turn left from a bridge over the Fontanka canal.

ll. 163–64, 'You come in the motley stripes/Of a milepost': this passage is about Blok. The striped milepost is a feature of the Russian landscape. Blok stands, a tragi-farcical figure, on the border of the nineteenth and twentieth centuries, between Tsarism and Communism.

l. 165, 'old as the Mamre/Oak': see Genesis xiv, 13, 24.

l. 182, 'Poets are blind to sin': Nadezhda Mandelstam has stressed that what fundamentally distinguished the Acmeists from the Symbolists was moral concern. 'The Acmeists renounced the cult of the poet and the principle that "all is permitted" to the man who "dares".' (*Hope Abandoned*)

l. 216, '*I am ready for death*': words spoken by Mandelstam to Akhmatova three months before his first arrest, for writing an anti-Stalinist poem, in 1934. The identities of Knyazev and Mandelstam are again blurred.

ll. 224–26. These lines, as B. A. Fillipov points out, are clearly inspired by the description of Kirillov in Dostoyevsky's *Possessed*, after he had hanged himself: 'In the corner formed by the wall and the cupboard, Kirillov was standing—and standing in a terribly strange manner.'

Across the Landing
Like Hedda Gabler's, Knyazev's suicide is an astonishing and irritating intrusion upon the busy scene, which is dominated by Sudeikina in her wild dance.

ll. 238–40, 'Isaac's': St Isaac's Square; 'the Dog': the Stray Dog.

l. 257, 'the head of Madame de Lamballe': the title of a famous poem by M. Voloshin, written in 1906, about a victim of the French Revolution.

l. 264, 'oceanic dance': the Russian adjective is 'okayanniy' (cursed); the pull of the English word, oceanic, which echoes the sound so closely, proved too much for this translator to swim against.

l. 271, 'Ivanushka of the fable' is a familiar character in Russian folklore. Usually, while his two bright brothers get married and get on, he sits on the stove and catches flies.

Part One, 2
Besides the goatlegged nymph, all the other roles mentioned in the introductory passage were associated with Sudeikina. Her husband painted her portrait in the role of the blunderer (Confusion-Psyche).

l. 283, 'Meyerhold's blackamoors': Meyerhold's production of Molière's *Don Juan* opened with a swarm of slave boys running on stage, lighting candles, ringing bells, etc.

l. 286, 'flayed the hide of the nation': Peter the Great built Petersburg on a swamp, at enormous cost in human lives.

ll. 291–304. The glory of Petersburg's musical and theatrical life is evoked, through the reference to Anna Pavlova dancing the Swan (Saint-Saëns–Fokine) at the famous Mariinsky Theatre; and to Chaliapin.

l. 306, 'the twelve colleges' corridor': the corridor of Leningrad University is noted for its exceptional length (1,500 feet).

Originally the building, begun by Peter the Great, housed twelve ministries ('colleges'). The poet, writing with her 'invisible ink', is doubtless alluding to the Soviet brand of education and culture —monolithic, 'straight'.

ll. 310–17. Akhmatova visited Paris in the spring of 1911, when Stravinsky's *Petrushka* was performed by the Ballets Russes and created a sensation. The ballet was performed in Petersburg in 1913. The 'yellow-black flag' is the imperial standard. The Summer Garden is the city's central park, beside the Neva. Tsushima is an island off Japan, where the Russian fleet was annihilated in 1905.

ll. 320–41. The shadows fly and Blok ('Mephistophilis or Gabriel') holds the stage alone. 'Demon with the smile of Tamara' refers to Lermontov's romantic poem, *Demon*; Tamara, a Gretchen figure, is destroyed by the Demon's kiss, but her soul is taken to heaven by an angel. Blok himself relates his gift of a black rose in his short poem, *In the Restaurant*; and reality and art are again confused in the reference to his Don Juan poem, *The Steps of the Commendatore*, which is a close parallel to the reality of Knyazev's entrance into the heroine's house before his suicide.

l. 355, 'O my blond-haired wonder'. Nadezhda Mandelstam's impression of her, ten years later: 'A nice, light-headed, flighty creature who had suffered much from hunger and other ordeals during the terrible years of Revolution.' (*Hope Abandoned*)

l. 365, the 'protected cedar' was at Komarovo, near Leningrad, a place much loved by Akhmatova. It is there that she is buried.

l. 370, the 'Maltese chapel' is in the former palace of the Voront-sovs in Leningrad.

Part One, 3

The poem's historical dimension is powerfully visualised in this section: the ominous approach of 'the existing/Twentieth Century' (i.e. from 1914).

ll. 440–53. The Cameron Gallery is a building at Tsarskoye Selo. 'All nine' refers to the nine muses. This tender reminiscence is addressed (according to Carl Proffer) to the critic N. V. Nedobrovo, Akhmatova's first love. It could equally be addressed to Gumilev.

Part One, 4

Mars Field is a large open area by the Neva, used for military parades. The house built by the brothers Adamini was one that

Akhmatova lived in for some years in the 1920s. The Church of the Saviour on the Blood was built in the late nineteenth century on the spot where Tsar Alexander II was assassinated. The church became a centre for anti-totalitarian thought in the period after the Revolution.

l. 471, 'On the road back from Damascus': Sudeikina was involved in a performance of a play called 'The Road from Damascus' at the Stray Dog. She is returning home from the cabaret with Blok. This is an excellent example of the fusion of literal precision and parable in the poem: for it is also a return into sin, as if St Paul changed back into Saul.

Part Two

Epigraph: 'My future is in my past'. Akhmatova's notebook refers to T. S. Eliot as the source. Shortly before her death she is said to have learnt that it was the motto of Mary Queen of Scots. It is intriguing that Akhmatova must have known Eliot's *Four Quartets*, in view of the similarities between the works: the musical form, the concern with time and history and the timeless soul; much of both works was written in cities under siege. That Akhmatova felt deeply for London's plight is attested by her poem *To the Londoners*: 'Time is now writing with impassive hand/ Shakespeare's black play, his twenty-fourth/ . . . Only not this one, not this one, not this one—/ This one we do not have the strength to read.' Eliot's poem is Akhmatova's English 'double'.

The reference, in the introduction, to *Requiem* first appears in one of the author's last revisions, near the end of her life.

l. 525, 'There were three': Blok, Kuzmin, Knyazev. Carl Proffer suggests Sudeikina, Blok, Knyazev, surely a misreading since clearly the first two must be celebrated poets.

l. 541, 'soft embalmer': this phrase, from Keats' sonnet *To Sleep*, is quoted in English in the Russian text.

l. 549. The Satanic figure is, again, Kuzmin (cf. ll. 109–19). Three poems by Kuzmin may provide a clue to his role in Knyazev's suicide. They are homosexual love poems to a young man, and two of them are dedicated to 'V.K.'. Both of these poems were written in 1912. The third poem, 'In sad and pale make-up', is addressed to a 'blond Pierrot' (cf. l. 393), whom the poet wishes to kiss endlessly. It is dated 1912–13. Beside any part he may have played in Knyazev's suicide, Akhmatova evidently finds his attitude towards it intolerable.

l. 561. Akhmatova's seventh book of poetry went with her in her evacuation from Leningrad during the siege. It never appeared in print. In the same plane was Shostakovich, with the score of his seventh symphony, 'the Leningrad'. B. A. Fillipov comments that the allusion may also encompass Beethoven's Seventh, which Akhmatova deeply loved. Once again, the deliberate blurring and mirror-effect is evident.

ll. 567–69, 579–84. In a note, Akhmatova writes—perhaps ironically—that the omitted stanzas are in imitation of Pushkin: who did indeed suppress stanzas for political reasons. The truth may be, I suggest, that originally the Soviet censors demanded cuts here before they would allow publication. We know that cuts were demanded—not surprisingly—in Parts Two and Three; she refused to publish these parts under such conditions. Perhaps later she saw how artistically effective these hiatuses could be. In them, 'silence itself speaks'.

ll. 595–96: Luga is a town near Leningrad; 'the land of the satin half mask' is Venice.

l. 601. *White Flock* and *Plantain* are early books by Akhmatova.

ll. 627–56. The author is for a moment afraid that her poem, which so obsesses her, is only another creation of the Romantic muse, that 'century-old enchantress'. But the muse protests that she has no ancestors. Despite the abundance of literary and artistic allusions, *Poem without a Hero* is, as Max Hayward has said, 'a conscious attempt to go beyond the Romantic poem. . . . Her main purpose is to recall an era in which there were no more heroes, only pseudo-Romantic masqueraders; the hero-individualist of the nineteenth century has come to the end of the road and his epigones (unless, like Knyazev, they died young) would be offered up wholesale to the Moloch of war and revolution.' Similarly the poem is not, as has been suggested, a regression to Symbolism: Symbolism 'was rooted, at the best, only in the imagination of its representatives. Akhmatova, on the other hand, was speaking not from imagination only, but from the depth of unimaginable experience.'

Part Three

ll. 687–700. Akhmatova's last double in the poem is mysterious. It is everyone who has perished in the labour-camps. But it is also her son, almost certainly: she does not know in what year he will suffer the most normal fate in those circumstances, death. She may also have in mind, again, her great friend and peer,

Mandelstam. Exactly when Mandelstam perished is uncertain to this day, though his widow believes it to be 27 December 1938. And Akhmatova's closeness and loyalty to him was remarkable; his death could not weaken the bond. 'We shouldn't be viewed as twins,' she used to say, 'but neither can we be separated: we go together.' For eighteen years, she and Nadezhda Mandelstam alone kept his poetry alive.

l. 693, 'the Noseless Slut': an obscure reference, perhaps death in the Stalinist era, faceless and indiscriminate.

l. 708, 'Hermitage halls': the Hermitage Museum of Art.

READ MORE IN PENGUIN

In every corner of the world, on every subject under the sun, Penguin represents quality and variety – the very best in publishing today.

For complete information about books available from Penguin – including Puffins, Penguin Classics and Arkana – and how to order them, write to us at the appropriate address below. Please note that for copyright reasons the selection of books varies from country to country.

In the United Kingdom: Please write to *Dept. EP, Penguin Books Ltd, Bath Road, Harmondsworth, West Drayton, Middlesex UB7 0DA*

In the United States: Please write to *Consumer Sales, Penguin USA, P.O. Box 999, Dept. 17109, Bergenfield, New Jersey 07621-0120*. VISA and MasterCard holders call 1-800-253-6476 to order Penguin titles

In Canada: Please write to *Penguin Books Canada Ltd, 10 Alcorn Avenue, Suite 300, Toronto, Ontario M4V 3B2*

In Australia: Please write to *Penguin Books Australia Ltd, P.O. Box 257, Ringwood, Victoria 3134*

In New Zealand: Please write to *Penguin Books (NZ) Ltd, Private Bag 102902, North Shore Mail Centre, Auckland 10*

In India: Please write to *Penguin Books India Pvt Ltd, 706 Eros Apartments, 56 Nehru Place, New Delhi 110 019*

In the Netherlands: Please write to *Penguin Books Netherlands bv, Postbus 3507, NL-1001 AH Amsterdam*

In Germany: Please write to *Penguin Books Deutschland GmbH, Metzlerstrasse 26, 60594 Frankfurt am Main*

In Spain: Please write to *Penguin Books S. A., Bravo Murillo 19, 1° B, 28015 Madrid*

In Italy: Please write to *Penguin Italia s.r.l., Via Felice Casati 20, I–20124 Milano*

In France: Please write to *Penguin France S. A., 17 rue Lejeune, F–31000 Toulouse*

In Japan: Please write to *Penguin Books Japan, Ishikiribashi Building, 2–5–4, Suido, Bunkyo-ku, Tokyo 112*

In Greece: Please write to *Penguin Hellas Ltd, Dimocritou 3, GR–106 71 Athens*

In South Africa: Please write to *Longman Penguin Southern Africa (Pty) Ltd, Private Bag X08, Bertsham 2013*

READ MORE IN PENGUIN

INTERNATIONAL POETS – A SELECTION

Octavio Paz Selected Poems
Winner of the 1990 Nobel Prize for Literature

'His poetry allows us to glimpse a different and future place ... liberating and affirming' – James Wood in the *Guardian*

Fernando Pessoa Selected Poems

'I have sought for his shade in those Edwardian cafés in Lisbon which he haunted, for he was Lisbon's Cavafy or Verlaine' – Cyril Connolly in the *Sunday Times*

Yehuda Amichai Selected Poems
Translated by Chana Bloch and Stephen Mitchell

'A truly major poet ... there's a depth, breadth and weighty momentum in these subtle and delicate poems of his' – Ted Hughes

Czesław Miłosz Collected Poems 1931–1987
Winner of the 1980 Nobel Prize for Literature

'One of the greatest poets of our time, perhaps the greatest' – Joseph Brodsky

Joseph Brodsky To Urania
Winner of the 1987 Nobel Prize for Literature

Exiled from the Soviet Union in 1972, Joseph Brodsky has been universally acclaimed as the most talented Russian poet of his generation.

and

Paul Celan	Selected Poems
Tony Harrison	Selected Poems *and* Theatre Works 1973–1985
Heine	Selected Verse
Geoffrey Hill	Collected Poems
Philippe Jaccottet	Selected Poems
Osip Mandelstam	Selected Poems
Peter Redgrove	Poems 1954–1987